QMC   318176 8

a30213 003181768b

D1429475

STUDIES IN ECONOMICS

Edited by Charles Carter
Vice-Chancellor, University of Lancaster

3

The Economics of Agriculture

The Economics of Agriculture

BY

MARGARET CAPSTICK

WITHDRAWN
FROM STOCK
QMUL LIBRARY

London
GEORGE ALLEN AND UNWIN LTD
RUSKIN HOUSE MUSEUM STREET

141616
HD 1434

First Published in 1970

This book is copyright under the Berne Convention.
All rights are reserved. Apart from any fair dealing
for the purpose of private study, research, criticism
or review, as permitted under the Copyright Act, 1956,
no part of this publication may be reproduced, stored
in a retrieval system, or transmitted, in any form or by
any means, electronic, electrical, chemical, mechanical,
optical, photocopying recording or otherwise, without
the prior permission of the copyright owner. Enquiries
should be addressed to the publishers.

© *George Allen & Unwin (1970)*

ISBN 0 04 631007 x *cased*
0 04 631008 8 *paper*

Printed in Great Britain
10 on 11 point Times Roman
by Alden & Mowbray Ltd
Osney Mead, Oxford

QUEEN MARY
COLLEGE
LIBRARY

Editor's Note

Economics is a large and rapidly developing subject, and needs, as well as elementary works for the beginner, authoritative textbooks on special subjects. This book belongs to a series of such textbooks (more than forty titles are planned): the general level is that of the second or third year in a British university course, but the books are written so as to be intelligible to other readers with a particular interest in the subject concerned.

C.F.C.

CONTENTS

INTRODUCTION

The purpose of this book is to provide an introduction to the special problems of agriculture in developed economies. Reference is made to conditions in developing countries where this is germane to the main scheme, but the detailed consideration of the place of agriculture in economic development is not attempted, since much of this is the province of development economics, and since the place of agriculture in developed economies makes much that is relevant and necessary in any discussion of developing agriculture superfluous in considering agriculture in western Europe and in the United States.

It is assumed that the reader will be familiar with the basic concepts of economic analysis, so these are in general used rather than explained.

Chapter II provides the factual background necessary to the analysis of agricultural demand and supply in Chapters III and IV, and of agricultural marketing in Chapter V. In Chapter VI the development of the present conditions of international trade in agricultural commodities is traced, and some of the problems of international trade are analysed and discussed. Chapter VII is devoted to a discussion of the main types of government policy towards agriculture, with special reference to the consequences of these policies for rural communities.

Statistical material has been provided by the Departments of Agriculture in several governments, and by the National Farmers' Union of England and Wales, who also made available their library. This help is gratefully acknowledged.

CHAPTER I

Some Types of Agricultural Organization

Agriculture is the occupation of a majority of the human race. The Food and Agricultural Organization of the United Nations estimates that, in the world as a whole, over 50 per cent of the population is engaged in agriculture, or dependent on agriculture for a living.[1] Among the countries of Africa and Asia only Libya, Japan, Cyprus, Taiwan and Israel have less than 50 per cent of their population engaged in agriculture, as farmers or farm workers, and in a few of the tropical African countries the proportion of the population so employed is over 90 per cent. Even in the world's industrially developed countries only Belgium, the Netherlands, the United States and the United Kingdom have less than 10 per cent of their economically active population engaged in agriculture.

It is very broadly true to say that the ratio between the agricultural and other sectors of the population of a country is proportionate to that country's stage of economic development. The African countries with over 90 per cent of their population dependent on agriculture—Mali, Niger, Ruanda, Burundi, Chad, the Central African Republic and Tanzania—are countries of very low income per head (less than one-twentieth of that in the United Kingdom).

Large areas of these countries have as yet no significant division of labour, and consequently no market economy; each family, extended family or tribe produces for itself the basic necessities of life—food, tree fuel and fibre or hides. Such countries have, in the strict sense of the word, subsistence agricultures. Small pockets of genuine subsistence agriculture remain in other parts of the world in remote and isolated communities; one notable example in the British Isles was, until the twentieth-century advent of the tourist ships, that of the Aran Islands off the west coast of Ireland, whose inhabitants provided all their own consumption goods from their fields, their livestock, and from the sea.

The advent of the trader, native or foreign, turns the subsistence

---

[1] FAO *Production Yearbooks*, Annual Series.

agriculturist into a commercial farmer. He may still be a very small producer, marketing no more in any one year than will enable him to pay interest on the loan that will tide him over from sowing time till harvest, or to pay his taxes. In bad years he will have no marketable crop, and will live as best he may on the produce of his holding. But once the habit of producing and selling agricultural commodities surplus to his own family's needs has been acquired, the farmer has ceased to be a subsistence farmer. He is more correctly described as a 'peasant' farmer, though the term 'subsistence' agriculture is sometimes loosely used to denote an agriculture where the marketable surplus is small and chancy.

Most of the world's millions of farmers are peasants. Taking the countries of Africa, Asia, Latin America and south-east Europe as a whole, the vast majority of holdings are small farms yielding a very low income to their owners or tenants; few, or no, mechanical aids to cultivation are used, and the total input into a holding may be seed, animal fertilizer (if it can be spared from other uses) and the labour of the occupier. The term 'peasant' has consequently acquired a pejorative meaning; urban dwellers use it as a generic term for ignorant and illiterate country dwellers. But peasant farming, in the sense of very small-scale farming, need be neither inefficient in its use of physical resources nor commercially negligible. The Japanese, whose typical farm is a family holding of one hectare, are technically advanced in the sense of using much fertilizer, improved strains of seeds, in making the maximum use of such machinery as is appropriate to their holdings (on its 6 million cultivated hectares Japan has $2\frac{1}{2}$ million small horticultural tractors) and in having developed a comprehensive system of agricultural co-operation and marketing and of agricultural education. Nor is peasant farming necessarily geared only to the production and marketing of a small, locally consumed surplus; Burma and Thailand for example are the world's major exporters of rice from their largely peasant holdings. About 55 per cent of the exports of Malaya are of natural rubber, two-fifths of which is grown on peasant holdings. None the less, one of the major problems of the developing countries is that of transforming inefficient peasant agriculture, with its uncertain contribution to food supplies and to economic growth, into an efficient agriculture capable of sustaining an increasing industrial population; agricultural advance may have to be preceded, as it was in Europe, by a revolution in both land holding and farm structure, though the experience of Japan again shows that this is not an absolute necessity.

In the developed countries of the West, and in New Zealand and Australia, farming is largely organized in family units; the farmer makes all the decisions, provides much or all of the capital, and does all, or a substantial part, of the manual work. The United States Department of Agriculture defines the family farm as 'a risk-taking business in which the operating family takes most of the risks and does most of the work'[2]—a definition which might equally apply to small shopkeepers or hoteliers, among others, and which emphasizes the fact that in much of the world the organizational problems of agriculture are more akin to those of the service trades than to those of industry. The United States family farm is one which provides full-time work for no more than three people, and so defined family farms account for nearly 75 per cent of all farm marketings in the United States, and over 50 per cent of those in the United Kingdom. A typical British family dairy farm of 60 hectares, worked by the farmer and one son, may represent a total landlord's and tenant's investment of £45,000 (about 108,000 United States dollars); in terms of investment per worker the British and United States figures of 45,000 dollars are roughly comparable.

Such a family farm is a sizeable business; much smaller farms predominate in some parts of Britain and the United States, in the Scandinavian countries and in the countries of the EEC. In Denmark, for instance, where small family holdings were created as a deliberate act of policy by the land reforms of the late eighteenth and early nineteenth centuries, as late as 1960 almost half the farms were of less than 10 hectares, and in the EEC 75 per cent of all holdings are still of less than 10 hectares. Family holdings are still being created as large estates are broken up by governments in such countries as the United Arab Republic, Italy and parts of Latin America. This is not being done purely for economic reasons; a class of independent small farmers is held to be a stabilizing element in a country's social edifice. Such nebulous concepts apart, it may be noted that in terms of technical and economic efficiency the family farm has been outstanding in many countries, from the minute holdings of Japan, which before the First World War fed a rapidly growing population and provided the major part of fiscal revenue as land tax, through the small farms of Denmark and the Netherlands, weathering years of agricultural depression in the late nineteenth century and again in the 1920s and 1930s by means of efficient stock management and marketing, to the substantial stock and dairy farms of New Zealand which are probably the best managed grassland farms in the world.

There are, however, drawbacks to family farming as a type of agricultural organization, the chief of which, as agriculture becomes more capital intensive, is that of financing land purchases and farm

[2] *Miscellaneous publication* No. 1023, USDA Office of Information.

operations; there is also some difficulty in achieving economies of scale which, though by no means so marked as in industry, are possible in some sectors of farming, notably in mechanical cultivations and harvesting and in some forms of intensive livestock enterprises. There have therefore grown up, especially in the United States, very large enterprises financed by joint-stock investment; California and Texas have cotton-growing enterprises of this kind, and in the United Kingdom there is at least one poultry business with several million hens which may be classified with these 'agrobusinesses'. The declining importance of manual labour as an input in all, and especially in arable and intensive livestock farming, will almost certainly lead to an increase in farming by private and public companies, but in this, as in other aspects of agriculture, prophecy is unwise.

Apart from the main stream of development of agricultural organization, which we may regard as a progression from subsistence to peasant farming to family farming to (possibly) agrobusiness, there are two other main types of farm organization. One is that of plantation agriculture. This developed from the seventeenth century onwards with the process of colonization, mainly in tropical and sub-tropical countries; it was characterized by large-scale production of a single export crop—tea, coffee, cotton, rubber, sugar cane—the capital being provided by, and the profits returned to, the colonizing country. Plantation agriculture is still of considerable importance; for instance, in Malaya two-fifths of the total cultivated area is in plantations, including over half the area of rubber trees. Plantation agriculture does not, however, accord with the political aspirations of many of the developing countries where it is found, and its importance is likely to decline.

The future of another form of large-scale farming, that of state farming, or collective farming under the aegis of the state, has also been doubted. It was established in the USSR in the 1930s, by force and terror, with unwilling participants who have had to be humoured into productive effort by the continuance of private peasant farming concomitantly with the growth of collective farms. Collectives were established in other Eastern European states after the Second World War. Their success has been variable, though some of their critics seem at times to hold collectivization responsible even for the vagaries of the weather. In some countries, such as Poland and Yugoslavia, collective farming has been modified. The increasing output of Russian agriculture in the second half of the 1960s and the undoubted efficiency of some East German collectives would suggest that the system is not inherently unworkable, and as the conditions for paid farm labour even on the medium-sized farms of the West approach more closely those of industrial workers it may be expected that some of the mystery which has surrounded the bond between the farmer and his own land and stock will disappear. Certainly the experience of the voluntary collectives, kibbutzim and moshiavim, of Israel, does not suggest that the rugged individualist is the only good farmer.

In an industry of such diverse organization, many features of which derive from accidents of history, and which is carried out in conditions of climate and vegetation which vary from tundra to tropical rain forests, any generalization is hazardous; whatever may be deduced from conditions in one place at any one time may be negatived by instances half a world away in space and in technology. Because of this great diversity, this book must deal primarily with the problems of agriculture in industrially advanced countries, though reference will be made to particular problems of types of farming elsewhere. As for projections in time, it is necessary only to recall that in the earlier half of the 1960s it was frequently assumed that Russia and China were now permanent customers for the grain surpluses of the West, and in 1966-7 it was assumed that India would be in permanent grain deficit. Stocks of grain in the United States, in effect world stocks, were drawn down to the lowest level which the United States Government considered compatible with safety of supply. Yet by 1968 stocks had mounted again to problem levels: Russia and China were no longer significant importers, and the Indian situation had rapidly improved. Two years of good harvests with improved varieties of plants have swung some of the prophets of famine into an equally exaggerated optimism about the food prospects of Asia, as if the monsoon were now guaranteed to be adequate and on time for ever more. Like the farmer, the agricultural economist operates under conditions of uncertainty, and should equally be wary of tempting providence.

With spatial and temporal qualifications very much in mind we may proceed to discuss factors of production in agriculture, the main determinants of agricultural demand and supply, the marketing of, and trade in, agricultural products, and the increasingly important role which Governments play in creating the conditions for agricultural production and decision making. It is also necessary briefly to consider some of the social problems which arise at a time of rapid change in agriculture.

B

CHAPTER II

The Factors of Production
in Agriculture

The classical economists differentiated three factors of production: land, labour and capital. These are still convenient headings under which to discuss the inputs in agricultural production; their relative proportions change spatially and temporally, and the use made of any one of them is dependent on the available quantities of the others, as well as on the general conditions of demand for agricultural products.

Problems of Factor Allocation

Suppose that a farm or a parcel of land is offered for sale. The neighbouring farmers, as well as possible buyers from a distance, will cast their eyes on it, and assess its possible value to them in the light of their command of the other two factors of production, labour and capital. Will they be able to work it with their existing machinery? If it was added to their present holding, would the existing farm buildings suffice to house the increased head of stock that the joint holding would carry? Or would a new set of buildings be needed, and how much would these cost? Would their financial assets extend to buying enough livestock to make full use of the extra land; or would it be better to put some of the newly acquired acres into arable, which needs less immediate capital outlay? Would the present labour force be able to cope with the extra work with existing plant; for example, would the present milking parlour be adequate for the milking of a bigger dairy herd with the present labour, or should there be two men to milk, or a parlour of a different design in which the present one cowman could milk the extra cows (in other words, could the productivity of present labour be increased)? Such questions show that *one* factor of production can rarely be considered in isolation; changes in one factor must be considered in the light of the availability of one or both of the other factors.

This first set of questions concerns the balance of factors. At any

18

one time, with given technology and given prices of inputs and of output, there will be one possible combination of factor inputs, either into an existing farm business or into a potentially expanded business which will be, for that business, the optimum combination or 'bundle'; this combination will produce the greatest possible margin of revenue over costs. With optimal factor allocation, the marginal product of each factor will be equal.

This concept has limited practical application; any change in the price of inputs or of output, or a change in the physical output of the farm such as might follow the adoption of a new strain of live-stock or of seeds may render the present optimum combination sub-optimal. A grain silo of optimum size at time t may be too small in year $t+2$. So an apparently sub-optimal choice of factor combination in year t may be the correct choice for the future development of the farm. Nor is it permissible to conclude that the combination of factors which suits one farm is necessarily the best for all, or even for any one other. Giles, with two stalwart sons whose aim is maximum physical efficiency in husbandry may well find that his optimum factor combination is one much more labour intensive than that of Hodge, who runs his holding extensively with no other labour than his own; their profits may be equal (Fig. 1).

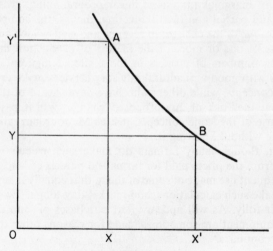

Fig. 1

A and B are alternative optimum combinations, since $OY^1AX = OYBX^1$. The isoquant on which they lie is an approximation to the actual process of substitution, which will proceed by discrete steps.

The second set of questions that arises concerns alternative uses for the purchase price of the land. Is the land really likely to add more to the profit of the farm than the interest charges on the money invested in it, and if so, will it add more to the farm profit than would the same money invested in some other form of production? Would it, for instance, be better to invest in an intensive house for pigs or poultry, which could be fed on the bought-in produce of someone else's land? Would the money be better spent on raising output from the existing holding, by drainage and increased use of fertilizer? Would it be better to invest the money in some land-using but non-agricultural enterprise, such as a caravan site? Or would it (and the nearer the farmer is to retirement the more often this last question arises) be better to invest the money outside agriculture altogether?

The second set of questions concerns alternative uses of a factor, and is therefore dealing with opportunity costs; the money may be invested *either* in land *or* in some other productive capital asset, and what it earns in land must be balanced against the income foregone from other forms of investment. The second set of questions is also concerned with marginal costing; in any form of investment, will income from the extra capital input exceed the extra cost?

Modern farm accounting makes use of the concepts of opportunity cost and of marginal analysis in linear programming, gross margin analysis and partial and total budgeting, that is, the comparison *ex post* or *ex ante* of the changes in revenue and costs which any change in the use of one or more of the factors of production may bring. Increasing numbers of farmers in the United Kingdom and other countries with good agricultural advisory services make explicit use of these concepts, while others who have never heard of them do in fact, when they ask of any proposed change 'Will it pay?', make implicit use of the same concepts, just as M. Jourdain talked prose all his life without knowing it.

In fact, though many farmers do make such calculations, it is obvious from the prices paid for farms and parcels of land and from the subsequent use made of some of them, that equally many farmers do *not* make such calculations, and market-day tongues wag happily over their folly. As will appear later, purchases of land and other capital equipment are sometimes made for reasons other than those of pure economics.

The Law of Diminishing Returns

Before we consider the factors of production separately, it is necessary to refer to the Law of Diminishing Returns, for this Law will be encountered in any discussion of land economics. It simply states that if the quantity of any one factor of production is fixed, the application to that factor of successive increments of the other factors will show progressively decreasing increments of production. The Law is often illustrated by the example of the application of successive units of labour to one hectare of land; there must come a point at which, if cultivations have been properly carried out, extra units of labour (hours of work) can only add fringe activities such as tidying up, and not add to output from the land at all. Practical applications of the Law are well known to farmers; if we have a cow fed on hay and roots and just maintaining her body weight, we may induce her to give a gallon of milk a day if we add to her food four pounds of a mixture of cereals and oil cake, but successive additions of four pounds of food will not produce successive extra gallons of milk; indeed, not only will the extra amount of milk given for each successive unit of food decline, but at some point, which will vary with her size and constitution, the cow will become ill.

In terms of profit the Law of Diminishing Returns may apply long before it begins to operate in physical terms; large parts of the grasslands of the British Isles are capable of much greater volumes of production than are now obtained from them, if more fertilizer were applied to them, and if more money and man hours were spent in controlling the grazing of animals. But though production could be greatly increased before returns per unit of fertilizer began to diminish in physical terms, the cost of the extra labour needed to intensify production from grass, and to look after the extra animals needed to utilize the extra grass, would in some cases be greater than the revenue which increased output would bring. The subsistence farmer may continue to apply successive units of labour to his holding as long as, by so doing, he obtains any increase in output at all; his need may be for maximum food production, and the fact that each successive hour of work increases output by progressively smaller amounts may be irrelevant to his calculations. The commercial farmer, however, must take into account the proper balance of factors, and will continue to increase his use of any one factor only to that point at which the revenue from each unit increase will equal its cost.

I. LAND AS A FACTOR OF PRODUCTION

In the present state of technology land is still a necessity for the provision of food for man and beasts. Food has been grown in laboratories without soil, but such production is improbable commercially in the immediate future. On the other hand, except for the arid deserts, the ice caps and the highest mountain tops, there is no land which, even if left uncultivated, does not grow food of some kind. Hence it was possible for Ricardo to speak of the 'original and indestructible powers of the soil', and to evolve the theory of rent from the consideration of the variations in production from the very poorest land, yielding bare subsistence for the cultivator and *no* surplus, to better land which could yield subsistence plus a surplus (rent) to the owner.

It has been estimated that there are between 1·4 and 1·5 billion hectares of land at present under cultivation in the world, and there are perhaps as much as 1·8 billion hectares in all suitable for cultivation. A further 2·8 billion hectares are in permanent meadows and pastures. This works out at 0·4 hectares (one acre) per head of cultivated land, and a further 0·8 hectares in managed pasture land. Europe and Asia, with only 0·6 hectares of total farm land per head are the most crowded continents, while at the other extreme Oceania has over 30 hectares per head.

It must be emphasized that the above figures of the estimated area of agricultural land are only estimates. In the absence of soil surveys the potential of some vast regions—Latin America, for instance—is simply unknown. There is, moreover, among agriculturists, no general agreement about the potential output of some of the world's presently unexploited soils, or even about the maximum physical productivity of apparently underutilized areas which are now farmed. The luxuriance of tropical rain forests may give a most misleading picture of what the productivity of tropical soils may be once the forest cover is removed, for in the absence of animal or chemical manure torrential rains may rapidly leach the mineral content of such soils so that within a very few years of forest clearance fertility may be exhausted. Unfortunately many of the undeveloped countries in which population pressure is becoming most severe are those with soil problems of this kind; if the need for food is such that small holdings growing the maximum output per square yard of vegetable crops must be established, it may be almost impossible to obtain enough manure to maintain soil fertility and structure. With adequate manuring and careful terrace cultivation continuing fertility may be achieved; in their absence the rivers of East Africa stain the Indian Ocean red with the eroded soils of the continent. The farmer has to learn how to work with, and sometimes how to work against, the physical and climatic conditions of his environment.

Misunderstanding of the basic properties and needs of land and their relationships to climate has led to a rapid deterioration of soils in some parts of the world. The dust bowls of the great plains of North America—a region which literally saw its top soil blow away—were created because it was not understood that ploughlands demand a minimum rainfall, and that, with less than this minimum, land should be left under grassland cover. Some of the range grazings of East Africa are being changed from lush grasslands to eroded wastes as, with the elimination of the tsetse fly and of natural predators, herds of cattle increase and overgrazing destroys the grass cover. The traditional farming practice of western Europe was that of some kind of rotation of crops and grass which maintained and, indeed, improved soil structure; in the United Kingdom mono-culture of cereals is a practice of very recent adoption, and in the late 1960s it has become clear that farmers of the heavier soils who practise it are experiencing difficulty in maintaining plant health and soil structure. It will be interesting to see whether these difficulties can be overcome without a reversion to traditional rotations.

Choice of land use varies with soil and climate in obvious ways; we do not expect to find orange groves on the moors of northern England or on the Canadian prairies, nor do we find temperate crops such as apples in African jungle clearings. Even within quite small distances land contours and microclimate make changes in land use advisable; hence the variety of the English rural scene. Favoured areas have the widest range of choice, and farmers there, having an absolute advantage in most forms of agriculture, will concentrate on those products for which their comparative advantage is greatest. New Zealand is probably, both in soils and in climate, the most versatile farming area of the world; as its land was settled in the nineteenth century its natural advantages over the old world both in arable and stock farming became obvious, and for a time it was an exporter of both grain and livestock. When the United States developed its grain exports to Europe, New Zealand concentrated on the production of meat, dairy produce and wool, for though it had an absolute advantage over the United States in both forms of production, its equable climate gave it a comparative advantage in livestock production.

Within the limits imposed by soil and climate certain other factors influence choice and intensiveness of production.

Location

The pioneer work on the location of agricultural production was that of J. H. von Thünen, *Der Isolierte Staat* (*The Isolated State*).[1]

[1] Von Thünen's *Isolated State*, trans. by Carla M. Wartenberg, ed. P. Hall, Pergamon Press, Oxford, 1966.

Von Thünen showed that around a market centre zones of production would develop, the inner zone being devoted to perishable crops, of high value per hectare, the outer zones being decreasingly intensively cultivated. Transport, both of agricultural output and of the chief inputs, is the main determinant of location in von Thünen's schema, as befits a work written in the days of horse transport. Countries of old settlement show the characteristic von Thünen patterns of agricultural land use; for instance, in Britain the Lea Valley was the area of horticultural production for the London market; cow dairies for the liquid milk supply were in the area surrounding the capital; less perishable foods—butter, beef—were produced in distant counties. The newer conurbations also developed satellite larders, but not so immediately on their doorstep, and in situations such as Evesham or the moss land of the Fylde coast, which show perhaps more of the influence of soil type than of market-centred location, for by the time they were growing rapidly, Britain had entered the railway age.

As transport developed through steam to the internal combustion engine, so the importance of nearness to the market declined. In the 1870s the United States and Canada became the granaries for the United Kingdom. Refrigeration made possible the development of New Zealand's trade in mutton and butter with the United Kingdom in the 1890s, and now gas storage of fruit means that the countries of the northern hemisphere can have apples and pears from Australia and New Zealand when home-grown fruit is out of season.

Canning and freezing of food has eliminated distance from the consumer market as a factor in location; it has, however, made nearness to the *processing* market of major importance, since quality demands almost hourly decision about the ripeness of the crop, and the time from field to freezer must be a matter of hours. So a horticultural area has appeared in sparsely populated north Lincolnshire because it was on Humberside that the freezing industry was originally developed to deal with fish.

Declining intensiveness of land usage with distance from the market was, therefore, a characteristic of the days of animal transport. Similarly on the farm, the substitution of mechanical power for horse or ox power has largely eliminated distance from the farmstead as a deciding factor in land usage. On the normal unfragmented British or American farm, choice of land use is usually made according to the peculiar properties of each field, whether it is wet or free-draining, whether its aspect is sunny or in some shadow, whether its contours are too steep for cultivation, what its place is in the rotation of crops or in the scheme of grassland management.

Dairy cows make an exception to this; where they must be driven to pasture they cannot reasonably be made to walk for more than about a quarter of a mile, and though the carting in of fodder to them can extend their area of land use, there has, as yet, been no evidence that this makes better use of the total area of a farm; consequently dairy farms still often show a pattern of concentric circles of land use, the cows' pasture fields surrounding the farmstead, the outer fields being in crops or grass for mowing, the outermost fields being used for the grazing of young stock. Within this roughly concentric pattern small areas of rougher or steeper ground make exceptions, and of course where the farm is small enough for cows to use the whole farm, there may be no discernible pattern of locational choice in field use.

In countries where fragmentation presents a problem, for instance in West Germany, where the average farm in the early 1960s was divided into eleven separate plots, location plays a major part in land use decision. Studies[2] have shown that the number of man hours spent on each plot, the amount of fertilizer used and the output of the plots declines with distance from the farmstead. Similarly in non-mechanized farming, such as that of western Ireland, the amount of manure that will be put on the arable plots will be decided by the distance that the donkey can carry it. Even in countries of larger farms there is a tendency for any separate plot of land to be less well farmed; hence the uneasiness with which farming neighbours view the sale of an adjoining field to a man from a distance; they fear that fences will not be kept up and that cattle will stray.

Location is still of overriding importance in some of the developing countries; the agricultural exploitation of parts of Africa and Latin America is delayed not only by deficiencies in techniques but by distance from possible markets and lack of means of transport to them. Production ceases at the point at which purely local needs are met.

Population Density

As long as transport acts as a constraint on marketing it is probably true to say that intensiveness of land usage varies with population density. Table I shows the ranking of twenty countries in order of population density and of gross agricultural output per hectare. The United Kingdom is an exception to the generally close correlation between both rankings because an industrial country which has large export markets can feed its population on the pro-

[2] Quoted in M. Chisholm, *Rural Settlement and Land Use*, Hutchinson University Library, London, 1962.

duce of the whole world: the position of Denmark, a major food exporter, is a correlative of that of Britain. In the years of British industrial supremacy, in the last quarter of the nineteenth century, the acreage of wheat grown in Great Britain declined from 1,400,000 hectares to 532,000 hectares, and, after a short-lived war time rise, to barely 500,000 hectares in 1931. The percentage of the country's agricultural land in permanent grass, which is usually an indicator of non-intensive land usage, increased from less than 40 per cent of the total area of crops and grass in 1870 to 60 per cent in 1938. Low

TABLE I. *Intensiveness of Land Use and Density of Population in Selected Countries*

Countries ranked by gross output per hectare	Population density and ranking (Persons per square kilometre)
1. China (Taiwan)	365 (2)
2. Netherlands	375 (1)
3. Belgium	314 (3)
4. Japan	270 (5)
5. Denmark	112 (12)
6. West Germany	233 (6)
7. Korea	302 (4)
8. Ceylon	178 (8)
9. Israel	129 (11)
10. Italy	174 (9)
11. France	91 (12)
12. United Kingdom	226 (7)
13. Indonesia	74 (14)
14. Thailand	64 (15)
15. Ireland	41 (16)
16. New Zealand	10 (18)
17. United States	21 (17)
18. India	156 (10)
19. Canada	2 (19)
20. Australia	2 (20)

Source: State of Food and Agriculture 1968, FAO, 1969
United Nations Yearbook of Statistics, 1968.

world prices for grain and oil cakes made United Kingdom farmers into processors of imported animal feed; many farms were little more than exercise ground for livestock. For quite other reasons— vast areas of land per head—the United States in this century has been able to survive agricultural practices prodigal of land. The output per hectare of cereals in the United States is still less than half that of the best European farming countries, yet production runs ahead of needs.

The Margin of Cultivation

The theory of Economic Rent explains the fact that at some point in each country agricultural use of land ceases: this point varies from place to place. The Connemara smallholder grows turnips and oats on land of a quality that his English cousin would regard as fit only for sheep grazing. He does so because he accepts as normal a standard of living that farmers on better land would eschew; the land of the quality that he cultivates yields subsistence only, and any better land would yield him an economic rent. To farmers in more fertile areas his land would be beyond the margin of cultivation; but to his forebears, traces of whose old cultivations can be plainly seen on remote headlands and high on the hillsides, his land would be well inside the margin of cultivation. It would have yielded them an economic rent.

The margin is therefore a shifting concept both spatially and temporally; marginal land is that land which at any one time and in any one place it just pays a farmer to cultivate. Physically the margin is clearly visible in hill areas between the managed grassland and the rough grazings. The marginal farm is that which it is just possible to operate as a commercial unit. In Britain the marginal farm is taken to be the farm on land whose commercial agricultural use is open to doubt; the concept of marginality also logically applies to the farm which is of doubtful commercial viability by reason of size, or because of alternative possibilities of land usage, but the term has an accepted meaning in agriculture, and 'marginal' land policies are those for land on the physical margin of cultivation.

Farm Size and Land Use

The *optimum* size of farm varies with the state of agricultural technology, the available labour force, and the availability of capital inputs other than land. The *minimum* farm size varies with the terms of trade between the agricultural and other sectors of the economy and the general standard of living.

As long as farming is labour intensive, and the terms of trade remain favourable to agriculture, as they do when a population is growing rapidly and it is not possible to import a significant part of food supplies, the minimum viable size of farm may remain very low, as it has done in Japan, where the average farm is still the family holding of 1 hectare, or in the United Arab Republic, where 90 per cent of the holdings are of 2 hectares or less; tiny holdings in densely populated countries like these are intensively cultivated. But as new sources of food supply become available, and as the standard of living improves with industrialization, the very small holdings will no longer provide an acceptable income; many Japanese farmers are now taking jobs in towns and leaving the farming of their holdings to the women. Similarly the typical Danish small farm of 10 hectares or less which was, until the 1960s, held up as an example of a type of prosperous family holding has, as other opportunities have opened to farm workers and as farm prices have failed to keep pace with costs, been given up and amalgamated with other farms; in the four years 1960–4, 21,000 such holdings, 23 per cent of the 1960 total, ceased to be separate units, and this process is continuing; between six and seven thousand Danish farms a year cease to be separate enterprises. However high the output per hectare, the total income from such small holdings is insufficient to provide a standard of living in any way comparable with that of industrial workers. So in most countries, as *per capita* incomes grow, minimum farm size rises.

Size of holding should not be confused with size of business.[3] A specialist livestock enterprise dependent on feed grown elsewhere can raise the income of a small holding to an acceptable level. Farms in which the output of the land plays a major part in production show a declining trend in income per hectare from the specialist dairy holdings through mixed farms and cereal growing farms to the extensively farmed livestock rearing and sheep holdings. If we take the minimum net income per farm to be no higher than that of the average manual worker, we find that in England and Wales the minimum viable size of farm goes up from the under 20 hectare group for dairy farms to the 60 to 120 hectare group for sheep farms.[4] In England and Wales holdings of less than 8 hectares, except for specialist horticultural holdings and intensive pig and poultry units are not generally counted as full-time farms. Only about half the agricultural holdings for which census returns are made are considered to be full-time farms.[5] Among these full-time holdings about 30 per cent are less than 20 hectares, that is, less than the minimum size which would be needed on any farming system largely dependent on production from the holding to give a total net return to the farmer comparable with the wage of a manual worker. Such a return clearly leaves no margin of funds for re-investment in the farm business.

[3] The United Kingdom Ministry of Agriculture classifies holdings in terms of estimated labour input, by 'standard man days', according to size, cropping, and head of livestock: this classification gives an estimate of size of business.

[4] *Farm Incomes in England and Wales 1967*, HMSO, 1968.

[5] *The Structure of Agriculture*, HMSO, 1966.

In spite of such obvious deficiencies, the farm structure of Great Britain is far better than that of continental Europe. In the EEC, for example, of the 6·4 million farms of over 1 hectare, 70 per cent are of less than 10 hectares, and only 3 per cent are of 50 or more hectares. In these countries the tendency to amalgamation of small farms is strong, as it is also in the United States, where the number of farms has been halved between 1940 and 1964, with the total area of land in farms slightly increasing. In the United Kingdom, on the other hand, the tendency to amalgamation is localized, being strongest in the problem hill areas of difficult physical conditions and relatively poor farm structure.

As farm size increases by the purchase of extra land the tendency is for output per hectare to fall; at the same time profit per farm increases through economies of scale in the use of labour and machinery.[6] Governments faced with the problems of low farm incomes and surplus production therefore may adopt policies of encouragement of amalgamation by annuities for farmers giving up their holdings and grants and loans for capital works needed after amalgamation. Sweden pioneered this type of policy; it has been successfully adopted by the Netherlands, and in 1967 the British Government introduced official financial encouragement of amalgamation by the Agriculture Act.

Conversely in developing countries where output per hectare is still of major importance either because present yields of crops are insufficient to maintain a secure food supply, or because agricultural produce is needed for export, it has been found that the creation of independent small holdings is a means to increase output. The United Arab Republic has, since the land reforms of 1952, had 90 per cent of its holdings in tiny plots of 2 hectares; its agriculture was already productive compared with that of many developing countries, but in the period 1950–4 to 1960–6 average yields of crops increased, that of cotton by 10 per cent and that of wheat by 31 per cent.

Forms of Tenure and Land Use

Individual holdings of land are not generally found in primitive societies where land is plentiful; tribal lands are extensively farmed, and it is not until population begins to press on land resources that individual holdings begin to be farmed, and division of labour makes possible the beginnings of commercial agriculture.

In more developed societies the evolution of forms of tenure has

[6] A. H. Maunder, 'Some Consequences of Farm Amalgamation', *Westminster Bank Review*, November 1966.

been dependent upon accidents of history. Where the break-up of the feudal system came early, as in England, the political ferments of the late eighteenth and early nineteenth centuries did little to undermine the economic security of the landed proprietors, and by the early nineteenth century enclosures had created estates of sizes varying between the thousands of acres of the biggest landowners to small estates of two or three farms belonging to the petty squires. So England had a system of leasehold tenure of farm land which lasted until the fiscal and financial pressures of the twentieth century caused the sale of many farms either to sitting tenants or on the open market. The British farm, owned or tenanted, was passed on intact to the eldest son. In the countries of continental Europe the break-up of the feudal estates was accompanied by the creation of small freehold farms, which, with subsequent subdivision among heirs, have become tiny and usually fragmented holdings.

TABLE II. *Yield of Wheat per Hectare, Yield of Milk per Cow, and Typical Form of Tenure for Selected Countries*

Country	Wheat yields kg/hectare* Average 1962–6	Milk yields per cow* kg Average 1962–6	Tenure
United Kingdom	40·8	3722	40% owner-occupied
United States	17·3	3639	57% owner-occupied
Denmark	41·7	3780	93% owner-occupied
France	29·9	2664	Mainly owner-occupied
Germany			
Federal Republic	33·8	3560	Mainly owner-occupied
Netherlands	43·8	4175	50% owner-occupied

* Estimated

Source: FAO *Production Yearbooks*, series: national *Agricultural Statistics*

It is impossible to establish any correlation between form of tenure and standard of farming, though it is often loosely said that the owner-occupier makes the best farmer because he is willing to take the long view and maintain his land and capital equipment better than the tenant, especially the insecure tenant. If we use yield of wheat per hectare and yield of milk per cow per year as proxies for intensiveness of land usage and standard of animal husbandry, we find (Table II) no correlation between these and form of tenure.

Some forms of tenure are, however, generally inhibitive of good husbandry. Over large parts of Asia, in the southern United States and parts of southern Europe, for example, share cropping occurs extensively. This is a system by which the landlord supplies the land and some or all of the fixed equipment, the tenant supplying the variable input and paying a share of the crop as rent. There is a theoretical explanation of the reluctance of the share cropper to maximize production; if the landlord has half the crop, the tenant, once he has produced enough to satisfy his basic requirements, will increase output only to the point at which marginal revenue = twice marginal cost since he will receive for himself only half of each increment of output; given diminishing returns to inputs, this will be at a lower level of output than that at which marginal revenue = marginal cost. Share cropping is thus held to be inhibitive of intensive land use; yet many efficient New Zealand dairy farms are worked on a 'share milking' basis, and the impoverished share croppers of the Nile Valley in the days before the land reforms of 1952 produced heavy crops of wheat, rice and cotton from land whose fertility had been maintained for centuries by their similarly impoverished forebears. This second example shows once more the overriding importance of population pressure, the supply of and demand for land, in determining intensiveness of land usage. But institutional factors may so operate that even in conditions of severe land hunger, such as obtained in Ireland when population increased by 50 per cent in the first half of the nineteenth century, land use may be extractive rather than intensive and conservative. Very few of the Irish were leaseholders; most were annual tenants, with neither security nor compensation for improvements. The most impoverished hired patches of 'conacre'—land let by eleven months tenancy to the highest bidder—on which, as indeed throughout the country, the monoculture of potatoes was practised, producing the maximum bulk of human food on a short-term basis. The famines of 1845 and 1846 and the subsequent massive emigration reduced the population, those remaining on the land being settled by the Estates Commission (now the Land Commission in Eire) on small farms which they purchased by annual payments. The removal of insecurity, of rack renting and of alien domination has outweighed the factor of population density in this case; the modern Irish freeholder uses the land better than did his insecure and impoverished ancestors.

Among leasehold tenants the secure tenant is said to be most likely to farm well. Absolute security of tenure is, however, neither widespread nor of long standing; the nineteenth-century English tenant farmer, who was, till the years of agricultural depression, a sound husbandman, was by no means secure in his tenancy, nor was he able to claim compensation for improvements made to his farm if he were given notice to quit. A series of Agriculture Acts, beginning with that of 1875, improved his position; from 1947 his tenure was terminable only by administrative certification of inefficiency, and by the Agriculture Act of 1957 he was given complete security as long as he paid his rent and did not farm in ways destructive of the farm's fixed capital. In Scotland, by an Act of 1968, a tenant's security of tenure has been extended to his heirs, unless the landlord can prove their total unsuitability to farm the holding.

Complete security of tenure for British tenant farmers has had paradoxical results. Where tenancies lapse on the retirement or death of the tenant, landlords, faced with the virtual impossibility of again obtaining possession of the farm once it is re-let, tend to sell farms on the open market with vacant possession. Otherwise, if they need to release capital from their landed investments they must sell farms to sitting tenants at prices much lower than they could obtain for farms with vacant possession. The British sitting tenant has a measure of job security unequalled in other industries; he may consent to vacate his farm in return for a golden hand-shake from his landlord, but he cannot be compelled to do so. Complete security of tenure has thus reduced the number of farms which are let.

Fortunately for landlords, the same Act (of 1957) which gave complete security to tenants also ended the freezing of rents at their average pre-war level which had done so much to reduce the return to investment in land in the 1940s and 1950s. A British landlord may now, with safeguards for arbitration if the tenant and he cannot agree, raise rents to the level which could be obtained for farms let by tender. During the 1940s and 1950s there was evidence that old-established tenants tended to farm less well than new tenants or owner-occupiers; with rents fixed at uneconomically low levels there was no inducement for tenants to maximize productivity, and there was insufficient return to landlords to enable them to maintain, let alone improve, the fixed capital of farms. British agriculture's average achievements lagged well behind those of Denmark and the Netherlands, where owner-occupiers and tenants alike had learned to farm well in the days of agricultural depression which lasted, with little intermission, from the 1870s till the Second World War. That average British standards of farming have now overhauled those of the foremost European countries is due to the greater stringency of economic conditions for farming in the 1960s; the need to pay adequate rents for farms has been one of the important changes that have had such striking effects.

One form of tenancy which has increased in recent years is that of the former owner who sells his land to an investment company and then leases back his farm on an agricultural tenancy. This is to some degree a result of the scarcity of farms to rent; as greater tenant security has made present landlords unwilling to re-let, so men seeking farms have been forced to buy, and the increase in demand has pushed up the price of farms to the point at which far too much capital is tied up in the land, and insufficient working capital is left. Sale and lease back is a way out of this difficulty, and it is certainly an increasing practice, though as nobody is keen to broadcast his sale of his farm, its extent is difficult to estimate.

Land Values

It may be asked why, if tenants are fixtures and capital is in-extricable, any private individual or public company continues to buy land as an investment.

This is a widespread problem. In most Western countries land prices have risen in the post war years much more steeply than have rents; for example in Holland the average price of farm land in 1940 was £200 per hectare; by 1960 this had risen to £750, the best land fetching prices of between £1,500 and £2,500 per hectare. While land prices had thus more than trebled, rents had only doubled, from £7·5 to £15 per hectare. A similar situation exists in the United Kingdom, where the comparative purchase price and rental values of farms are shown in Table III.

TABLE III. *Index Prices of Farm Land and Rents,*
1939 to 1963

	Farm land prices		
Year	With possession	Let	Rents
1939	100	100	100
1955	252	218	172 (1956)
1963	541	627	301

Source: D. R. Denman, 'Land Ownership and The Attraction of Capital into Agriculture', *Land Economics*, Vol. XLI, 1965.

The price of tenanted farms bought as an investment had in the period risen more than six times, doubling in real value; this was proportionately more than the rise in prices of farms sold with vacant possession for occupation and use, and twice the rise in rents. In the United States the price of farm land rose by nearly 100 per cent between 1954 and 1964, a rise in real terms of about 160 per cent.

C

Colin Clark[7] has estimated the economic rent of land, that is the residual income to land, being the gross product after deducting payments to all other inputs into agriculture, for various periods from 1867 to 1966. This is not to be confused with actual rents paid; in times of agricultural depression it has been well below cash rents, since these tend to remain stable for existing tenants while returns to farmers fall. In the depths of the agricultural depression in the 1880s the return to land fell to zero. Only in the 1930s, when land prices were very low since expectations about the future of agriculture were understandably gloomy, and in the years of agricultural prosperity and generally low interest rates after the Second World War, was the return to money invested in land higher than to the same sum invested in government securities. In the 1960s, though the economic rent of land has increased, the attractiveness of land as an investment has declined as interest rates have generally risen. The study from which Table III is taken established the return to land on 133 English estates totalling 56,000 hectares at 1 per cent net of maintenance.

Why, then, do investors still look for land? In the United Kingdom the problem is complicated by the incidence of taxation, especially of estate duty payable on the death of the owner, for landed estate attracts lower rates of duty than do other types of investment. In the United States it is still possible to buy land as an expense to set against income from other sources. Real values of land have risen steadily, and the owner who can let land bought for £625 per hectare at rents which give him a return of 4 per cent on his investment with forms of tenancy which leave the tenant responsible for most repairs to fixed capital, is probably doing rather better than investors in popular forms of equity stocks, such as unit trusts. Land, like sound equities, is a growth stock, and will normally have an annual yield less than government and comparable securities. This is an old problem; Trollope's worldly archdeacon a hundred years ago invested in land though it brought in only $2\frac{1}{2}$ per cent because 'It is a comfortable feeling to know that you stand on your own ground. Land is about the only thing that can't fly away'.

The effect on the would-be owner-occupier of the attractiveness of land as a long-term investment is, however, not so happy. It may be a comforting thought to existing owners that money invested in land is well hedged against inflation, but the capital value of land does not pay current expenses, and high interest rates (creeping up through the 1960s from 7 per cent to 10 per cent) make the purchase of farms for commercial use a doubtfully economic investment.

[7] Colin Clark, 'The Value of Agricultural Land', *Journal of Agricultural Economics*, 1968.

It is often evident that too much of the financial resources of farmers is invested in land, leaving too little working capital; so the purchase of extra land sometimes fails to raise total net output by the amount needed to cover interest charges on the purchase price. The economics of the purchase for owner-occupation of mediocre farms at £750 per hectare are beyond reasonable explanation at interest rates prevailing in 1968–9; this represents a notional rental charge of £30 per acre (£75 per hectare). The net income per acre in the cropping farms included in the British Government's Farm Management Survey, the most profitable group of farms, is £13 per acre (£32·5 per hectare). A notional rent of £4 18s per acre (£12·25 per hectare) must be added to this to obtain the net total income of the average owner-occupier. How the gap between this net income and interest charges on land is bridged is a mystery; it must be assumed that the owner-occupier farms and lives at a very low standard, hoping that when he retires capital appreciation will repay his mortgage.

Small farms in favoured areas will no doubt continue to be bought at prices high in relation to their potential income yield, for reasons of amenity, but the family farm of 20 to 60 hectares (in United Kingdom conditions—other European countries may have a smaller norm for a family farm) will probably lose its attractiveness for buyers if interest rates remain high. The structural effect of high land prices may therefore be a polarization of farm structure between the small farm handed down in the family, and escaping the worst effects of death duties by its small size, and much bigger units into which institutional and commercial owners are reorganizing their estates as tenancies lapse. The 1960s may, unless there is a general fall in interest rates, unaccompanied by a fall in the profitability of farming, prove to have been the heyday of the owner-occupier.

Alternative Uses for Land

Agriculture is the largest user of land, but almost everywhere it is being increasingly encroached upon by urban development. Table IV shows the change in the proportion of the world's population living in cities since 1800.

In the densely populated industrial countries the demand for land for urban uses is accelerating; in England and Wales, for instance, an average of 10,800 hectares of agricultural land was lost to other development (building, industrial uses, roadmaking and so on) in each year from 1900 to 1960; the estimated loss per year is now about 20,000 hectares (0·17 per cent of the whole), and this land is of better than average quality because urban growth is continuing most rapidly in the very areas where towns first developed because enough food could be grown locally to feed their populations. The same process is at work in other developed countries such as the United States. Urban development is a much more intensive user of land than is agriculture; one hectare of land with an agricultural value of £700 would be worth ten times that amount for housing development in an English provincial town, and much more again in a large city; so as improved transport makes possible the spread of urban activities—industrial dispersal, or commuter travel—values for land suitable for non-agricultural use rise.

TABLE IV. *World Population and World Urban Population, 1800–1960*

Year	World population (millions)	Percentage of population living in cities
1800	906	3·0
1850	1,171	6·4
1900	1,608	13·6
1950	2,400	29·8
1960	2,995	31·8

Source: N. Lichfield, 'The Scale and Pattern of Future Urbanization'; Paper from the 22nd Oxford Farming Conference, 1968.

Piecemeal policies for the control of land use have been adopted in many countries; in European countries these are confined to rural areas which, because of low incomes to farmers, or unemployment, or out-migration, or fragmentation of farms, are in some way problem areas. The United States approaches land use from the point of view of soil classification and conservation needs, under which heads it has classified all land: policy is to prevent soil-exhausting land use, not to decide optimum use of land. The United Kingdom, where there has been since 1947 a policy for town and country planning, has no overall classification of land, and land-use policy; local authorities are the planning areas and the final arbiter of land use is not the Ministry of Agriculture but the Ministry of Housing and Local Government.[8] The increasing yearly gross output of agriculture—that of United States farms increased by 26·5 per cent between 1958 and 1967, and that of the United Kingdom by 36 per cent—makes it unlikely that an overall policy for land use will be considered necessary in the foreseeable future. Nor have the centrally planned economies evolved a system for evaluating optimum land usage,

[8] Now part of the Ministry of Local Government and Regional Planning.

though Soviet economists have concerned themselves with methods of so doing.[9] Land is still generally regarded as expendable.

II. LABOUR AS A FACTOR OF PRODUCTION

General Problems of Labour in Agriculture

Agriculture differs from most of industry in several respects which make its problems of labour use unique.

First, in any form of agriculture proper (as opposed to the processing through animals of feed grown elsewhere) there is a seasonal peaking of the work load at harvest time and to a lesser extent at sowing time; this problem is unlikely to be eliminated until remote control of tractors, now in the experimental stage, is perfected. There are various ways in which this problem may be partly solved.

A labour force big enough to deal with the work peaks may be kept on the land; this means that for a large part of the year labour is under-employed, as it is alleged to be in some developing countries. The provision of suitable employment for surplus labour in the off-peak seasons is a problem of any largely rural society; in some places such labour is needed in maintaining capital works necessary for agriculture, such as irrigation channels; in other places work is found by government for seasonally surplus agricultural labour in the provision of public utilities—hence the excellence of the minor roads in the west of Ireland.

A second solution is the diversification of farm enterprises. The sowing season may be extended by the growing of corn, roots and greencrops which have different lengths of growing period; this will stagger the harvest period also. The traditional British and European farm with its corn sowing, root sowing and thinning, hay harvest, corn harvest and root-pulling would have a busy season extending from March to November, after which the stock would be indoors and need daily feeding. The increasing practice of specialized farming has diminished the importance of this means of spreading the work load.

A third solution is the use of casual labour; the United States still has nearly 200,000 migrant agricultural workers who spend a substantial part of the year in harvesting work, mainly in fruit and vegetable harvesting. In the United Kingdom such seasonal work is largely done by housewives; men with full-time jobs elsewhere also do a considerable amount of seasonal work in such jobs as haymaking.

[9] J. Wilczynski, 'Towards Rationality in Land Usage under Central Planning', *Economic Journal*, Vol. LXXIX, September 1969.

A fourth possibility is to employ contractors. This is a useful supplement to regular labour for maintenance work such as ditching, hedge cutting, fencing, sheep shearing and so on. For most seasonal work it is, however, not so useful; no one who has had experience of chasing an agricultural contractor on the one day that all the neighbourhood has hay ready for baling can accept that contract work is a satisfactory solution. Farmers are sometimes criticized for buying machinery which they can use only for a few days in a year, but until we can control the weather such apparent over-capitalization will be necessary.

The second big difference between agriculture and industry is in the size of the unit of production. Very many farmers employ only one man, and very few employ more than two or three men. When one man leaves, the farmer may be faced with the loss of 50 per cent of his total labour force. He then must choose between intensifying production to make possible the employment of a replacement at ever-increasing wages, or cutting back production to the point at which he can manage all the work of the farm single handed. The latter may be very difficult, especially when money is borrowed and interest must be paid; in these circumstances the farmer's wife tends to become the unpaid farm worker.

Sometimes it is possible to employ a part-time worker in place of a full-time employee. Part-time workers from industry are increasingly important as full-time workers leave agriculture; a study in Northumberland[10] has shown that farmers in the south of that county where there are industrial towns are better supplied with labour than those of the remote rural north of the county; this is because farm workers near the towns can change jobs without migrating and are willing to work seasonally or part-time in agriculture, whereas those from the remote areas who leave farming leave the district altogether. In the United Kingdom as a whole the proportion of part-time to all agricultural workers has increased from 21·5 per cent in 1950 to 28·5 per cent in 1968.

As agriculture becomes technically more complex, the usefulness of such part-time labour will diminish; it is not possible to replace the modern young adult British farm worker, who will not only have several years' practical experience of work with machinery or livestock, or both, but have had, at farm school or by day-release classes, a technical training comparable with that of an industrial craft or technical apprentice, with the first man from the factory bench who wants some extra cash. The straw-chewing rustic of

[10] Northumberland Agricultural Executive Committee, reported in *Farmers' Weekly*, October 1969.

urban mythology was never typical of the British farm worker, who commanded a range of skills in the care of livestock or in field work that demanded intelligence and care. As the proportion of the part-time agricultural labour force which is composed of ex-farm workers who themselves have such skills diminishes, the difficulty of adjusting need for labour to changing technology and size of enterprise may be expected to increase.

Changes in the Agricultural Labour Force

Farmers, their wives and families and hired workers compose, in proportions that vary with time and place, the agricultural labour force. In continental Europe, the United States, and in the greater part of the agricultural sector of less developed countries, family workers outnumber hired workers; Britain is exceptional in having had a hired labour force bigger than that of family labour, but even in Britain the proportions are rapidly altering to more nearly those of the rest of the developed world.

TABLE V. *Proportion of Family and Hired Workers in the Agricultural Labour Force in Selected Countries*

Country	Year	Labour Family (a) %	Hired (b) %	Year	Labour Family (a) %	Hired (b) %
United Kingdom[11]	1954	30·0	70·0	1967	40·0	60·0
United States	1954	77·6	22·4	1967	82·5	17·5
Denmark	1950/4	48·6	51·4	1965	69·5	30·5
EEC	1954	70·0	30·0	1964	79·2	20·8

Column (a) = farmers.
Column (b) = all employed full-time workers.

[11]British Agricultural Census statistics do not differentiate between farmers' families and other hired labour; nor do the statistics of the Ministry of Employment and Productivity. The official figures for the hired labour force are thus those for all labour other than that of farmers and their wives. Parish studies have shown that the ratio of non-family workers to family workers is in some cases as low as 1:6. There are areas of the country where no local juvenile labour other than that of farmers' sons is entering agriculture; the juvenile entry consists in these areas entirely of farmers' sons and pre-college students who are doing the year's farm work which institutions of agricultural education consider to be necessary and sufficient to provide a background of agricultural practice. The outflow of hired workers from British agriculture is, therefore, certainly higher than official figures would suggest, and the juvenile entry is lower. The high proportion of farmers' sons included in the figures for hired labour may explain the apparently low rate (less than 50 per cent) of unionization of the agricultural labour force: no doubt there are disputes between farmer and son, but they are unlikely to be of the kind that the trade union official can solve.

In the developed world total farm population is falling rapidly. In general the productivity of labour in agriculture is well below that in industry or the service trades; consequently earnings in agriculture are also low (Table VI). But we may note the anomolous

TABLE VI. *Agricultural Output as a Percentage of Gross National Product, the Agricultural Labour Force as a Percentage of Total Labour, and Agricultural Earnings (Wage Workers) as a Percentage of Earnings for Manual Workers, 1966*

Country	Agricultural proportion of GNP	Agricultural proportion of labour force	Agricultural earnings as percentage of earnings of manual workers
United Kingdom	3·5	3·5	75
United States	4·0	6·0	50
France	7·3	19·8	—
Germany			
Federal Republic	3·8	13·4	50
Netherlands	6·8	10·7	60

Source: National Agricultural Statistics; *UN Yearbooks*

position of the British farm worker who is as productive as the average worker in the country (and therefore more productive than workers in some industries) but who is still at the bottom of the wages structure. This is partly a matter of tradition; the agricultural worker always has been ill paid and an improvement in his earnings commensurate with his productivity would set off a round of wage claims from all other sectors of the economy. Partly also the low earnings of agricultural labour reflect the industry's structure; an increase in profit margins which would allow the 40 per cent of farmers who employ labour to pay wages comparable with those in industry would also increase profits for the 60 per cent of farmers who do not employ labour. The latter are the small farmers, a decline in whose numbers is probably inevitable in conditions of surplus production. And, thirdly, low returns to labour are part of the whole problem of less than average returns to total factors which is one of agriculture's perennial problems discussed below (pp. 53–4).

Between 1954 and 1967 the numbers of all workers employed in agriculture in Britain, Europe and in the United States declined as shown in Table VII. Other factors besides the earnings differential which induce the outflow of labour are the general prosperity and

TABLE VIIA. *Outflow of Labour from Agriculture in the United Kingdom and the United States, 1954 to 1967 (thousands)*
(Includes farmers, full-time and part-time family and hired workers)

	1954	1967	Percentage change	Annual average change, percentage
United Kingdom	1,035	705	−32·5	−2·5
United States	8,651	4,903	−43·3	−3·3

Source: Annual Review and Determination of Guarantees 1969, HMSO. *Agricultural Statistics* 1968, USDA.

TABLE VIIB. *Outflow of Labour from Agriculture in the European Economic Community, 1960 to 1965 (thousands)*
(Includes farmers, full-time and part-time family and hired workers)

	1960	1965	Percentage change	Annual average change, percentage
Germany	3,623	2,970	−18·0	−3·6
France	4,029	3,370	−16·3	−3·3
Italy	5,850	4,950	−15·4	−3·1
Netherlands	429	356	−17·0	−3·6
Belgium	257	208	−19·1	−3·8
Luxembourg	21·9	18·7	−14·5	−2·9

Source: European Communities, Joint Information Service, *Newsletter No. 8*, 'The Agricultural Labour Force in the EEC', June 1968.

growth of the economy[12]—workers will more readily move to other jobs outside farming if such jobs are easy to come by and seem to be secure—the accessibility of other work, and differences in conditions of employment. The latter are often deciding factors; the weekly hours of work in farming are typically longer than in industry (about 17 per cent longer in the United Kingdom), some work is

TABLE VIII. *Increase in the Annual Productivity of Agricultural Labour in Selected Countries*

Country	Years	Annual productivity increase percentage
United Kingdom	1949–59	5·9
United Kingdom	1959–68	6·0
United States	1940–64	6·0
EEC	1954–64	6·0

[12] K. COWLING and D. METCALF, 'Labour Transfer from Agriculture: A Regional Analysis', *Manchester School of Economic and Social Studies*, March 1968.

inevitable at weekends and on public holidays, and the married worker very often lives in a tied house, which will be cheap and nowadays will usually be comfortable, but which limits his mobility and is therefore resented. Movement out of farming typically takes place at the age of mobility (when boys can obtain a driving licence) and on marriage, when the earnings differential is felt more severely.

As labour leaves agriculture the productivity of the labour that remains increases (Table VIII). A good hand milker can milk six to eight cows an hour (uncomfortably), but in a modern milking parlour he may handle over 50 cows an hour comfortably; two men with a tanker combine-harvester and lorry can cut, thresh and carry home four hectares of grain in three to four hours: the same area cut by a binder, stooked, and carried home by horse and cart would occupy two men and the whole farm household for days, while the threshing would be a full day's hard work for farm men, family and all the neighbours. The increasing productivity of labour is thus dependent on an increasing supply of more, and more powerful and efficient machinery, and the limit to the release of labour from farming may be reached not because of any technical limit to labour replacement but because of the inability of agriculture to generate sufficient capital to finance such labour replacement.

The process of decline in the agricultural labour force must at some point cease; it is not possible to produce food without any labour at all. There is, unfortunately, no means of telling, apart from trial and (possibly) error, whether this point has been reached for any particular market for agricultural produce. There are always interested prophets who can point to neglect of land and fixed equipment as the first signs of falling standards of farming that must lead to falling output. This may well be true of some farms, but if the agricultural sector as a whole continues to increase output there seems to be no reason why the rest of the community should be concerned. So far the process of adaptation of the farm labour force has been continuous. Technical improvements increase output beyond the increase in demand; there is a constant pressure on profit margins; the paid workers go to better paid and less onerous jobs in towns; next the younger members of the farm household leave, then the occupiers of holdings that are marginal because of situation or size. During this process the farm labour force ages; for instance, in the United Kingdom more than two-thirds of the insured workers who left agriculture between 1960 and 1965 were under 40 years old; with a much reduced juvenile intake the agricultural work force thus has an inbuilt tendency to decline, even if economic circumstances do not induce this in the future.

The process of adaptation is not, however, smooth and painless. The farm worker who is within reach of urban employment may make the change easily enough, but the worker from the remote rural areas must migrate. As the rural population dwindles so the disadvantages of rural life—inadequate transport, too small schools, distance from shops, from entertainment and from work for young people—become more irksome. In parts of rural America and Europe the population is too scattered to form an adequate society. The small farmers who remain in these areas are in many ways socially underprivileged; their attachment to their farms and to a (possibly illusory) feeling of independence, makes them willing to accept for a long time a standard of living and social provision much lower than they could obtain as hired workers elsewhere.

In many countries, among which Sweden was a pioneer, policies for the assistance of the transfer of labour from agriculture, especially from the remote areas, to other work have been in operation since the 1950s. These take the form of grants or annuities to farmers who give up their holdings for amalgamation with others, for forestry, recreational areas, or other uses. The number of holdings under 20 hectares in Sweden had fallen by 42 per cent from 1951 to 1966, and total agricultural production has been adapted to a target of 80 per cent self-sufficiency in food instead of the previous 95 per cent target. The farmers and workers who move out of agriculture are given training for other jobs.

Similar schemes are operated in most other West European countries; in Holland, for instance, a more general scheme of assisted withdrawal from agriculture has been responsible for about 2,000 farm amalgamations a year. By the Agriculture Act 1968, the British Government has also adopted a scheme of assisted amalgamation; the success of this, which aims at a re-structuring of agriculture into larger units, may depend on the availability of capital—it is no use offering a grant of part of the capital costs of reorganizing two farm units into one if the owner of the new unit cannot borrow the rest on economic terms.

The most recent and far-reaching plan for withdrawal of labour from agriculture is that produced by Dr Sicco Mansholt for the European Economic Community.[13] Recognizing that 80 per cent of the farms in the EEC are too small to provide work for even one man, Dr Mansholt's plan aims at a reduction of the work force in farming from the 12 million at which it stood in 1964, to between 5 and 6 million in 1980. This is to be achieved by schemes for the assistance

[13] Commission of the European Economic Community, Spokesman's Group, *EEC Projections and Plan for 1980*, Brussels, December 1968.

of early retirement, re-training, farm amalgamation and reorganization, as in schemes already operating in some problem rural parts of the EEC. In addition there is to be an attempt to cut back the grossly inflated dairying sector by substantial headage payments for the slaughter of dairy cows, where a farmer undertakes to have all his cows slaughtered and to give up dairy farming.

Whether such wholesale transference of labour will reduce the surpluses of agricultural (especially dairy) produce which present problems for the EEC may be doubted; the minimum size of farm aimed at—40 cattle, or 60 hectares of grain—is well below the limit at which economies of scale cease to operate. The evidence of the United States and the United Kingdom does not suggest that transfer of labour in itself will solve the problem caused by production outstripping demand. If the OECD forecasts of surpluses of all agricultural products (except beef) in the developed countries prove correct in the 1970s, there may have to be withdrawal of other factors of production, besides labour, from agriculture. In this process of adjustment agricultural labour must expect, however much its productivity increases, to continue to receive less return than it might obtain elsewhere.

Economies of Scale in the Use of Labour

As labour leaves the land, as farms become fewer and bigger, and as more capital is invested in machinery, fixed plant, and purpose-built farm buildings, certain economies of scale in the use of labour will be possible; this has already become noticeable in the intensive production of poultry, eggs and pigmeat; specially designed buildings with automatic feeding of the animals and removal of dung make it possible for one man to look after hundreds of pigs or thousands of poultry. It is because of developments in these sections of the industry that the overall increase of the productivity of labour in agriculture has been so high since the mid-1950s. Similar economies of scale in other livestock enterprises are less likely; though the United States has successful 'beef lots' of several thousand cattle each, cows have more complicated nutritional requirements than pigs or poultry, and dairy cows especially need individual attention if they are to be healthy and productive. The evidence so far is that when dairy herds much exceed one hundred cows, the number that one man can reasonably milk and look after, economies in labour can be outweighed by loss of efficiency of supervision and the need for duplication of plant. Similarly there is not yet evidence that arable farms become more efficient in their use of resources when they pass the 200 hectare size; increased size above the optimum only means duplication of machinery and, perhaps, too little managerial supervision.

There is thus, as compared with industry, limited scope for economizing on labour use in agriculture by increasing the scale of production, but the possibilities of increasing labour productivity as compared with the present situation are immense; there is no practical limit when we talk in terms of an *optimum* herd size of 100–120 dairy cows, and note that the *average* size of a dairy-herd in West Germany is six cows, that in the Netherlands it is twelve cows, and in England it is still only 30 cows. In Britain and the EEC as a whole there are a very few areas (East Anglia and northern France being the most important) where an appreciable proportion of arable farms approaches the optimum size. Whether existing farms can be regrouped into production units of optimum size is dependent on the availability and on the opportunity cost of capital; here again it is not possible realistically to consider one factor of production in isolation.

Agricultural Education and Training

We have hitherto discussed labour in agriculture as if labour were a homogeneous factor; it is, however, obvious that the seasonal fruit picker is not the equal in skill of the man who can look after 100 dairy cows, or handle a 16 foot cut combine-harvester. Training in agricultural skills has traditionally been given on the farm, but the need for greater understanding of the underlying principles of machinery maintenance and livestock management, together with proper methods of farm recording and business management, have made necessary a general increase in agricultural training (in specific skills) and education (in underlying principles). This is generally the sphere of government sponsored services; proportionate investment in agricultural research, education and training varies broadly with the stage of technical efficiency of agriculture. Canada, the United States and the United Kingdom all put more than 50 per cent of their total agricultural intellectual investment into research; Denmark and the Netherlands are exceptional in that, being technically as efficient as any other countries, they still place the major emphasis on education and advisory work. Both are countries where the efficiency of small farms is vital to the total economy.

There is probably no one optimum allocation of resources between research, education of the next generation of farmers and advice for the present generation. At any one point of time there are vast numbers of farms which are applying very little of the results of research that have been proved in practice; one striking example is the sorry state of much British grassland, where the basic principles of optimum management were established in the 1930s, but where general standards of management fall far below those that obtain in other sectors of agriculture. A good agricultural adviser can do much, but the best disseminator of research results is the farmer who successfully applies them. This usually (not always) means the educated farmer, and the raising of the general and technical level of education in rural areas is one certain way of improving the efficiency of agriculture.

In the United Kingdom the emphasis in agricultural advisory work has in recent years moved somewhat from the simple encouragement of technical efficiency and is now, by means of a scheme for grants for the keeping of approved records, being placed on business efficiency and the optimum allocation of resources. The results of such recording schemes, unless meticulous attention to daily entering of transactions is observed, may be misleading, and conclusions about the allocation of resources which may be derived as national (arithmetic) averages from dubious data are not to be taken seriously. In present European conditions of over-supply of agricultural products, however, any moves towards impressing on farmers the need for a cool look at their factor inputs per unit of output are to be welcomed. It had been a criticism of earlier advisory work that inevitably the advisers, in helping individual farmers to maximize income, also tended to bring about a general increase in production when this was possibly against the ultimate best interests of farmers as a whole.

Agricultural education has become both more technical and more specialized. Farm schools and apprenticeship schemes turn out young people highly qualified in a restricted range of skills, and their best prospects for advancement are in these more specialist occupations— poultry keeping, pig management, machinery maintenance and so on. When such young people find that there is little opportunity for advancement in the small production units of agriculture, and that they are probably earning only about two-thirds of the wages of their contemporaries in factories and in skilled trades they tend to move out, sometimes into agriculture's ancillary industries as mechanics, salesman and the like, and sometimes away from the industry altogether into unskilled but more lucrative employment. This continual movement of trained agricultural workers into other occupations represents a considerable transfer payment from agriculture to the rest of the economy. Those workers who remain move to the bigger farms where they can become specialists in one field.

This, in some respects desirable specialization, has unforeseen effects; it may be necessary for the maintenance of soil structure and for the control of disease that livestock fed on grass should be included in the rotation of operations on the cereal cropping farm; it may even be desirable that sheep should alternate with cows in grazing on the all grass farm; yet it is uncommon to find among younger agricultural workers a sufficiently wide range of skills to make such flexibility of operations possible. The industry has thus twin problems; the need for training and the provision of a ladder of opportunity demand the development of specialist skills; the need for flexibility of operations demands the old-time farm worker who could turn his hand to anything from arable work through maintenance work to stockmanship.

Managerial Skills

The farm worker may be trained to understand individually most agricultural operations, but the skills of management are less easily taught. Co-ordination between technique and finance, deployment of the work force, day to day and hour to hour decisions on cultivations, make demands on the farmer which he is often not able to fulfil. The question of the desirable structure of agriculture is inseparable from that of the supply of able managers; many a farmer does very well on his own, yet is quite incapable of organizing work to a time table such as a hired worker will insist upon; thought should be given to the supply of managerial talent when schemes for minimum-sized farms which will entail the universal employment of labour are put forward.

The demonstration of a new technique, a new machine, or the potential of a new breed of livestock is a comparatively simple matter. This type of demonstration is the stock in trade of agricultural shows, open days at agricultural colleges, farmers' discussion groups and the like. The mental flexibility needed for the constant adaptation of management to make the best of new techniques and changing circumstances is probably, however, best fostered by raising the general level of education of farmers. This is particularly important in developing countries where agriculture must adapt quickly if resources are to be released for industrial development. In already developed countries it is the more highly educated farmer who is usually most ready to make use of advisory services, management consultants and so on, and then, if necessary, to modify and adapt their advice to his own circumstances.

III. CAPITAL AS A FACTOR OF PRODUCTION IN AGRICULTURE

The word 'capital' is commonly used in two separate but related meanings; first, it is used to denote the durable physical materials used in the productive process. These are, in agriculture, principally land, buildings, fixed plant, machinery, stocks of consumable physical inputs such as fertilizer, feeding-stuffs and unsold produce; livestock are also an important part of the capital of farming. Secondly, 'capital' is used to refer to the financial means of acquiring these media of production, that is to money owned or borrowed.

Physical Capital

It is traditional to distinguish two kinds of physical capital in agriculture:

1. Landlords' capital; this is the land itself, with buildings, fences, drains, watercourses and so on.

2. Tenants' capital; this means removable physical inputs such as tenants' fixtures (milking machines, electric motors for instance); machinery such as tractors, forage harvesters, combines and a host of smaller machines and tools; livestock, and all the non-durable physical inputs.

Landlords' Capital

Legislative control of the relationship between landlord and tenant has in some case blurred this distinction; for example, in the United Kingdom landlords are, since 1958, no longer responsible for the maintenance of farm fixed capital, apart from the roofs and main structures of buildings, and farms are let on 'full repairing leases' by which tenants must assume much of the landlords' former responsibility. Complicated legal provision is made for the assessment of the state of the physical capital of the farm at each change of tenancy, and for the mutual compensation of landlord and tenant for any deficiencies.

The role of the landlord has changed in other ways; the tenant no longer asks his landlord for new buildings, hoping that they will be provided out of the landlord's own resources without a rise in rent (though willing to accept the necessity of the latter after a long bargaining process). Instead it is usual for the landlord to provide necessary new fixed equipment at a pre-agreed rate of interest (usually 2 per cent above Bank Rate) or for the tenant to provide the new equipment himself, with the landlord's agreement to take it over at a valuation at the end of the tenancy. The landlord is still therefore in a strong position to influence farming practice; he can refuse either to provide or to take over any fixed equipment which he considers unsuitable to the farm—for example, a cow shed which will hold far more cows than the farm is capable of supporting—and this 'prudent landlord' principle has been adopted as a criterion for financial assistance with capital projects by the British Agricultural Land Service. Owners of large estates, especially institutions, usually encourage investment by progressive tenants, but small landowners may not have either the means or the inclination to do so.

The distinction between landlords' and tenants' capital is highly artificial: for an owner-occupier there is no such division. It is, however, useful to separate the function of land ownership, some of the peculiarities of which have been discussed, from the ownership of movable capital. Land has, except for comparatively small areas in regions of urban development, little opportunity cost, but other physical capital, or rather the financial investment in it, has, and its use in agriculture must be compared with other possible uses in the economy.

Land itself as a capital input is remarkable, as we have seen, for its low current rate of return as an investment, and its potential growth value. Because of the latter characteristic it is the best security for obtaining funds to invest in other physical capital. In the United States registered mortgages amounted to about 29 per cent of the total value of farm real estate in 1967; about three-quarters of all sales of farm land involved some form of credit, and 72 per cent of total purchase price of all farms is now borrowed. There are no comparable figures for the United Kingdom; the largest institutional lender is the Agricultural Mortgage Corporation, a government-assisted body which derives its funds from the issue of public debenture stock, but its total mortgages outstanding in March 1968 were, at £103·1 million, only about one-sixtieth of the total estimated value of farm land in England and Wales. There is much private lending of money on the security of first mortgages on land, both by institutions and by individuals.

Tenants' Capital

In the post-war years there has been an enormous increase in the amount of physical capital other than real estate in all except the most primitive agricultures. Concomitant increases in output have been made possible by the use of more fertilizer, and more livestock are kept to process the greater amount of fodder into consumer goods such as meat and dairy products. Machines are not only more numerous; in technically advanced agricultures, where the number of some types of machines has fallen (as manpower declines, for instance, so the number of tractors that it is possible to utilize declines) the power and complexity of machinery is increasing. The cutter-binder for corn was replaced by the tractor-drawn combine-

D

TABLE IX. *Changes in the Numbers of Agricultural Tractors on Farms in Certain Regions, 1948–52 to 1966*

	1948–52	1966
Europe (excl. USSR)	969,224	5,243,625
USSR	595,000	1,660,000
North America	4,043,419	5,538,562
Asia	36,656	236,535
Oceania	161,736	406,065

Source: FAO *Production Yearbook*, 1967.

harvester; this in turn is giving way on the larger farms to the self-propelled combine. Developments in the conservation of grass have been even more striking; a farm which in the 1930s might have harvested its grass crop with a reciprocal blade mower, two simple turning machines, three or four horses and carts and many hand rakes and forks may now have a total of £15,000 invested in grass harvesting machinery, silage tower and electrically operated automatic feeding machinery.

Consequently the annual investment in machinery and fixed capital in modern farming systems has increased till the investment ratio for agriculture (the investment in fixed assets expressed as a percentage of gross output) is comparable in Britain with that in manufacturing industries. At constant prices the gross fixed capital formation of British agriculture increased by 40 per cent between 1957 and 1967; that of industry increased by 25 per cent.[14] In the same period expenditure on agricultural machinery (new purchases and maintenance) increased by 25 per cent, showing a shift in emphasis from the mechanization of field operations to mechanization of work at the farmstead. The solid legacy of the eighteenth century in buildings and yards is gradually being replaced by modern concrete structures which make possible greater economies in labour.

It is these continuing additions to, and improvements in, fixed and other capital which have made possible British agriculture's comparatively large increases in labour productivity. It is, however, very doubtful whether similar increases can be maintained as employed labour declines; the small farms have already shed all their paid labour, and further increases in productivity must depend on the re-structuring of the industry into larger units. This in turn must depend on the availability of suitable fixed capital; the buildings

[14] *National Income and Expenditure*, HMSO, 1968.

which at present are adequate for two 20 hectare farms will be totally unsuitable for one 40 hectare holding. The provision of sufficient new capital will depend on the ability of agriculture to provide finance either out of its own savings or from borrowed funds.

Financial Capital

It is not only the increasing amount and value of physical capital that make the supply of credit for agriculture important; most farm products have a production period of months or years, and the farmer has to live and to be able to meet production expenses until his crops or livestock are ready for market. Lack of such short-term finance at fair rates of interest is one of the major problems of agriculture in developing countries, where farmers are often at the mercy of merchants or money lenders who charge exorbitant rates of interest because of local monopoly lending powers, or because the farmer, once indebted, cannot free himself.

The normal source of capital in developed countries for industrial or other enterprises is the new issue market. There are, however, few public companies in European farming, and even in the United States the agrobusinesses are many times outnumbered by small family enterprises; consequently the ability of agriculture as a whole to borrow in this way is limited. Farmers have themselves to arrange finance from whatever sources they have access to, where they can establish their credit-worthiness.

In the past the chief sources of finance for farming have been farmers themselves and their landlords; the farmer has relied on his savings to provide working capital—machinery, feeding-stuffs, fertilizer and so on—and on his landlord to provide fixed capital. We have seen that the role of the landlord has changed, and that where he provides new fixed equipment it is at rates of interest comparable with those that the tenant would pay elsewhere. Savings, given a high marginal rate of taxation, are not easily made; farmers are now, therefore, more dependent than formerly on their own borrowing power, and this must depend not only on the past success of their enterprise but on the opportunity cost of money invested in agriculture.

In developed economies the main source of financial capital for farmers is now the joint stock bank; in the United Kingdom bank loans to farmers have increased from £70,880,000 in 1946 to £513,700,000 in 1968, about 9 per cent of all bank advances. This total represents thousands of individual transactions in which local bank managers, under general rules about total lending from their head offices, make individual assessments of the credit-worthiness of their customers. There are in Britain no special banks whose function is to lend to farmers. In Europe and in the United States such special banks, government assisted or co-operatively owned by the farming community are almost universal; to the borrower these provide the great advantage of credit at subsidized rates of interest, while to the lender they represent a secure investment, since risk is widely spread, loans are made on the basis of local knowledge of the borrowers, and administration is supervised by government agencies. The United States Farm Credit Administration and the French National Agricultural Credit Bank are the apexes of two such locally based credit organizations.

Besides supervising and subsidizing the loan operations of co-operative banks, governments provide finance for agriculture through special credit organizations; such are the British Agricultural Credit Corporation, which guarantees bank loans for agreed farm improvements, and the American Farmers Home Administration, which advances money at fixed interest rates to farmers who cannot obtain loans through the usual sources. There are also, in almost every country, government grants and loans for a very wide range of farm improvements and improvements of the rural infrastructure, such as roads, electricity supplies, water supplies and so on.

In terms of total outlay on an approved project there may be little to choose between the system of *ad hoc* government grants and the system of subsidized low interest rates; if interest is fixed at a rate 30 per cent below the current commercial level this is equal to a grant of 30 per cent. Obviously the value of the fixed interest loan increases with every increase in the interest rate for loans from commercial banks: British farmers balancing the current 10 per cent interest costs of marginal investment against the probable marginal revenue may look with envy on the 4 to 7 per cent interest rates of United States rural credit institutions. There are some fields of capital investment—purchases of livestock, feeding-stuffs, fuel and other working capital—to which British Government grants do not, in any case, apply. Over the whole field of capital investment the British farmer is probably less subsidized than his counterpart elsewhere; in approved capital works, certain livestock enterprises (beef calf rearing), fertilizer purchases, he probably has equal help, but the young man starting to farm will find subsidized non-tied credit more generally useful.

Banks and governments are the most important institutional lenders to farming; there are others whose relative importance it is not possible to estimate accurately. Families are still the source of much farming finance; parents and brothers and sisters may leave money invested in a farm, often at rates of interest advantageous to the farmer, especially where the farm is owner-occupied and the risk of total loss of capital is negligible. There are, too, many non-family private loans and mortgages arranged; the Radcliffe Committee estimated total farmers' indebtedness in the United Kingdom to such private lenders at £405 million (at a time when total commercial bank loans to agriculture were about £400 million).

In recent years the importance as lenders of feeding-stuff manufacturers and merchants has increased in some types of agricultural enterprises; feeding-stuffs for broilers and pigs, for example, may be supplied on credit by merchants, with a contractual arrangement for payment when the mature product is sold. There are more elaborate extensions of this type of contract which go beyond more credit facilities into the sphere of vertical integration. More generally merchants do not formally lend to farmers; they merely wait for payment of bills, and the farmer by delaying payment loses the discount offered for settlement of accounts within a month. Estimates of the average rate of interest represented by loss of discount range from 12 per cent to 20 per cent, so the farmer who can keep clear of trade debt and presents himself to his bank manager as a creditworthy customer is in a relatively favourable position.

The Return to Capital in Agriculture

The total return to capital in agriculture covers the return to land as well as to other capital investments. We have seen that, because land is held for a variety of reasons, not all of which are comparable with the reasons for other commercial investment, it is misleading to include land as a factor of production on the same basis as other factors in assessing the total return to investment in agriculture. It is usual, therefore, to include a notional rent for land in the expenditure side of the balance sheet for an agricultural enterprise; this should put tenants and owner occupiers on an equal footing for comparison, but in fact it is a very imperfect method; the old established tenant of a non-maximizing landlord may still, in Britain, be paying a rent of £7 10s per hectare; a new tenant may pay £20 per hectare. An owner-occupier of an unencumbered property may have no rental-equivalent outgoings (maintenance apart); a new owner may have a mortgage repayment of £58 per hectare ($14\frac{1}{2}$ per cent on two-thirds of the purchase price of the farm). All calculations based on notional rents and averages must therefore be treated with the greatest reserve; within the range of possible rates of return there will be some farmers who are obtaining from their investment in their farms at least as much as they could obtain in any other possible investment, while others will be barely able to service their borrowings and eke out some sort of living. It is the latter who 'live poor to die rich'; they hope that at the end of their farming life the increased sale value of their farm will enable them to meet their commitments and have some surplus on which to retire.

From both British and United States farm costings[15] one thing stands out; it is only the biggest farms in certain types of production (cropping in Britain and cotton and wheat production in favoured areas of the United States) which are yielding a 10 per cent return on invested capital apart from land, and leaving the equivalent of a manual workers' wage for the manual and managerial work of their occupiers and their wives, which may be regarded as the necessary minimum for living expenses. For smaller farms, especially those engaged in livestock enterprises, the *total* net return is less than a 10 per cent return on capital; the return to manual and managerial work is negative: such holdings cannot provide both a reasonable standard of living and also funds for re-investment.

The Mobility of Factors of Production in Agriculture

Industrialists typically expect a return of 15 to 20 per cent on investment; the farmer may well ask why if, as in Britain, he is making at least as efficient use of his capital and labour, in terms of physical output, as his industrial compatriot, his return should be so much less. Fortunately for the rest of the community, farmers do not, on the whole, think in these terms. J. R. Bellerby estimated in the mid-1950s[16] that the gap between the incomes of farmers and those of the rest of the community had to be as wide as 20 per cent before farmers even became aware of it; his historical analysis of agricultural and other incomes in the years between the two world wars led him to conclude that the supply price of farm enterprise was, comparing farms with firms with a similar scale of operations and similarly uncertain conditions, not more than 50 per cent of the supply price of industrial enterprise.

It is doubtful if some of the factors impeding the mobility of farming enterprise which Bellerby listed operate today in developed societies. Children no longer grow up in rural fastnesses where they know of no other possible life than farming; they are less likely to be seriously disadvantaged by differences in education in seeking other employment; and as incomes in general increase, so the rural

[15] *Farm Incomes in England and Wales, 1967 and series*, HMSO. *Agricultural Statistics 1968, and series*, United States Department of Agriculture, Washington.

[16] Bellerby, J. R., *Agriculture and Industry: Relative Incomes*, Macmillan, London, 1956.

advantage of some lower food costs become less. But it cannot be doubted that there is still considerable 'stickiness' of factors of production in agriculture; partly this arises from the farmer's attachment to his home and to a feeling of independence, partly from a genuine liking for outdoor life, even if the charms of this pall in midwinter storms or midnight attendance on animals, and partly from a barely conscious feeling that the farmer never has to justify his activities; individually he may be only adding to the United States Commodity Credit Corporation's stocks of wheat, or diluting the British Milk Marketing Board's pool price for milk, but he knows, if he ever gives any thought to the matter, that his is one occupation that can never be entirely superfluous.

This 'stickiness' of the factors of production may seriously hamper a country's economic development, as long as agriculture is, as it is over most of the world, less productive in its use of resources than the rest of the economy. Once equality in productivity is reached, the advantages of transfer become less easily demonstrable. Farmers and farm workers from predominantly rural areas do not tend to leave their farms to go into chemicals, electronics, or one of the more technically advanced industries. They typically move into transport, construction and service trades; those with a good deal of capital retire. The occupational inertia of farmers may, once the productivity of factors in agriculture reaches the average national level, be a disguised transfer payment from agriculture to the rest of the community.

CHAPTER III

The Demand for Agricultural Products

The demand for agricultural products is derived ultimately from millions of consumer choices. The characteristics of this demand vary according to the time scale and the behaviour of the first buyers of agricultural commodities. It is therefore convenient to consider demand under three separate time-period categories.

Long-term Demand

In the very long term, changes in the amount of food consumed reflect secular changes in population. As population has grown, so throughout much of the world agriculture has expanded output to meet increased demand (Table I).

TABLE I. *Indices of Regional Per Capita Food Production* 1948–52 to 1966*
(Average of years 1952 to 1956 = 100)

Region	1948–52	1966
Western Europe	86	120
Eastern Europe and USSR	87	142
North America	99	104
Oceania	102	121
Latin America	98	100
Near East	93	107
Far East (excluding China)	94	104
Africa	95	97

* Calorie basis

Source: FAO *Production Yearbooks.*

The very areas, however, which show the fastest growth of population are those (Latin America, Africa, parts of Asia) where food production has not kept pace with population growth, and these are all areas in which population increases must be expected over the next few decades to exceed those of the developed and well-fed countries both absolutely and proportionately (Table II).

Looking well ahead, therefore, farmers can expect the need for their products to increase; whether this need will be effective demand on world markets depends on the development of the economies of the now poorer countries, and on future patterns of world trade. Japan, for instance, as she has industrialized, has become a major importer of food; increased purchasing power abroad might allow other countries whose own agricultures now barely support their peoples to follow her example. Before this can happen there will be a period of time in which these countries may not be consumers of food produced elsewhere, or only in times of domestic crop failure. Whether the now developing countries can ever enter world food markets as buyers is so much dependent on the willingness of the

TABLE II. *Average Annual Percentage Increase in Population by Regions*

Region	1952 to 1966 percentage increase
Western Europe	1
Eastern Europe	1·7
North America	2·2
Oceania	3·0
South America	4·0
Near East	3·6
Far East	3·0
Africa	3·4

Source: FAO *Production Yearbook*, 1967.

developed countries to accept manufactures from the poorer countries that it is impossible to predict, solely on the untypical example of Japan, that the growing populations of the undeveloped world will ever be effective customers for the surpluses of food which the Western world is capable of producing. It is quite possible that improvements in technology in their own agricultures will enable them to support their populations on the mainly cereal diets to which they are accustomed. So, though we can predict that secular increases in population shift demand curves to the right, we cannot predict to what products or in what markets these demand curves will apply.

What we do know is that in general as incomes rise so the type of food preferred changes; a nation of underfed rural and urban poor

TABLE III. *Co-efficiencies of Income Elasticities of Demand by Major Food Groups, Expressed in Terms of Quantities*

Food group / Area	Cereals	Starchy roots	Sugar	Veget-ables	Fats and oils (including butter)	Milks and milk products (excluding butter)	Meat	Eggs	Fish
Area									
North America	−0·5	−0·7	0·0	0·3	0·0	0·08	0·4	0·02	0·3
EEC	−0·3	−0·3	0·5	0·6	0·16	0·3ᵃ	0·7	0·8	—
Mediterranean countries	−0·3	0·0	0·8	0·4	0·5ᵇ	0·8	1·1	1·1	0·5
United Kingdom	−0·4	−0·3	0·0	0·5	0·02	0·09	0·4	0·3	0·2
Japan	−0·17	−0·15	0·8	0·5	1·1ᵇ	2·0	1·7	1·0	1·5
Argentina and Uruguay	−0·3	−0·2	0·3	0·6	0·35ᵇ	0·4	0·15	0·1	0·4
Other Latin America	0·14	0·1	0·4	0·55	0·8	0·85	0·75	1·1	0·5
Near East and Africa	0·2	0·1	1·2	0·7	0·8	1·1	1·3	1·3	1·0
Asia and Far East (excl. Japan)	0·5	0·16	1·3	0·9	1·2	—	1·5	2·0	1·1
No. of medium (0·5 to 1·0) elasticities	1	0	3	7	3	2	2	1	3
No. of high (1·0 and over) elasticities	0	0	2	0	2	2	4	5	2

ᵃ Including butter.
ᵇ Excluding butter.

Source: FAO Commodity Review Special Supplement, *Agricultural Commodities Projections* for 1970, Rome, 1962.

will, in the first stages of development, spend the greater part of its increments of income on food, mainly on cereals. When appetite is satisfied increasing real incomes lead to a demand for more varied food; if we study Table III we find that while only the poorest countries, at the time of this investigation, still had positive income elasticities of demand for cereals and starchy roots, nearly all countries had moderately high or very high income elasticities of demand for meat and eggs; sugars and fats are intermediate products. National preferences disrupt the pattern of change; the Japanese have an exceptionally high demand for fish, the Asians for eggs.

It would be rash to predict that present patterns of change in demand will necessarily continue; if the American processors of soya beans can condition consumers to like imitations of beef and bacon (analogs) and the oil companies can develop commercial quantities of synthetic proteins matured on petroleum derivations, then the world meat shortage which is predicted for the 1970s and 1980s may not materialize. Some farmers, however, whether cattle feeders or growers of soya beans, will have to feed the millions of extra people who, unless present demographic projections are completely awry, will be in the world by the year 2000. The total demand for food will be increased in the long term.

Producers of non-food agricultural commodities may find that the demand for their products diminishes with the availability of substitutes; the production of synthetic rubber, for example, has increased rapidly since the war; in the period 1953–5 it accounted for 37 per cent of total consumption, and by 1965 for 62 per cent, and during this period the price of natural rubber fell to 50 per cent of its 1955 price. Wool and cotton have similarly suffered from the competition of synthetic fibres. It is impossible to predict what new products may emerge and what the long term conditions of demand may be for non-food agricultural products.

Medium-term Demand

The farmer plans production not for the needs of people as yet unborn, but with an eye on the markets for his products next year, or a few years ahead. Crops with very long production periods—tree crops particularly—are planted more in faith and hope than in any knowledge of what demand conditions will be when the crop is mature. Most calculations of future demand relate to the medium term, in which it is possible to make some estimates of probable changes in consumption. In the medium term total demand for food depends on the size of the population which each food market supplies, and on the per capita real income of consumers. Population projections are not notably reliable; in Britain, for instance, the Royal Commission on Population which reported in 1949[1] concluded that over the fifteen years to 1964 'The number of annual births will almost certainly decline': by the year 1977 they expected the population of Great Britain to begin to decline absolutely. Now the population of Great Britain is expected to be, by the year 1981, about 59 million, or 20 per cent higher than it was in 1949. Until recently estimates of the future size of the population were higher than this; now the birth-rate is expected to continue its recent decline. But who can tell whether this will be so as the children of the two post-war birth-rate 'bulges' produce their own families?

To somewhat speculative projections of population we must add other projections of the rate of growth of incomes; we do know that as incomes rise above mere subsistence there is a tendency for the proportion of the increments which is spent on food to decline. This means that as a nation as a whole increases its income, total food expenditure declines as a proportion of that income (Table IV). But

TABLE IV. *Expenditure on food as a Percentage of all Consumer Expenditure, 1957 and 1966*

Country	1957	1966
Belgium	31·0	25·5
France	33·0	29·0
Germany		
(Federal Republic)	40·0	37·5*
Italy	40·5	38·0
United Kingdom	30·0	25·0
United States	22·4	19·0

*Includes beverages and tobacco.

Source: *United Nations Yearbook of National Accounts Statistics*, 1967

this tells us nothing much about absolute food expenditure; high food prices will mean that a higher proportion of income is spent on food; a very unequally distributed national income will have a less proportion spent on food than an evenly distributed income; in the United Kingdom in 1967 the highest income groups spent less than one-fifth of their incomes on food, the poorest spent one-third.[2]

[1] Report of the Royal Commission on Population, Cmnd. 7695, HMSO, 1949.
[2] Department of Employment and Productivity, *Family Expenditure Survey*, 1968.

There is a limit to the capacity of the human stomach, and though total food expenditure of the rich is much higher than that of the relatively poor the increase is in type and quality of food, not in

TABLE V. *Food Expenditure According to Income Groups: Households of two Adults and one Child: United Kingdom 1968*
(shillings per week)

Food/Income	£10 and under £20 (1)	£25 and under 30 (2)	£40 and Over (3)	(1) as a percentage of (3)
Bread	7·52	7·25	6·44	116·5
Potatoes	4·22	4·09	3·91	107·5
Margarine	0·83	0·88	0·68	122·0
Sugar	2·73	1·98	2·03	74·3
Meat	25·69	31·91	39·69	64·7
Milk	9·70	10·59	13·24	73·2
Butter	3·30	3·68	4·08	80·8
Meals away	7·19	13·00	30·04	23·9

Source: Department of Employment and Productivity *Family Expenditure Survey 1968*, London, 1969

absolute quantity. The greatest inequality between the expenditure of different income groups in the United Kingdom is not, as might have been expected, in beef or poultry or fruit but in meals eaten

TABLE VI. *United States Per Capita Consumption by Major Food Groups, 1960 and 1967* (retail weight equivalent pounds)

	1960	1967
Meat	146·7	157·7
Poultry	34·5	46·3
Fish	13·2	13·6
Eggs	42·5	41·4
Dairy products	384·0	369·0
Fats and Oils (excl. butter)	48·9	51·3
Fruit, fresh	89·4	80·3
Fruit, processed	50·2	51·8
Vegetables, fresh	150·1	141·8
Vegetables, processed	50·4	58·1
Flour and cereal products	147·0	142·0
Sugar and other sweeteners	108·8	112·5
Coffee, tea, cocoa	15·4	15·1

Source: *Agricultural Statistics*, USDA, 1968

away from home, where the farm-gate value of the food is a very small part indeed of total expenditure. The higher income groups eat much more fruit, vegetables, meats and milk; they eat less bread, sugar and margarine (Table V).

Medium-term predictions of demand for any one country must to a large extent be based on present patterns of consumption. In the countries with high per capita incomes the proportion of total expenditure on goods and services which goes to food is now less than 25 per cent; in the United States it is 18·1 per cent, and in the United Kingdom 23·5 per cent. This proportion has fallen steadily since the war and must be expected to decline. But total per capita food consumption has nevertheless increased. It is tempting to predict that changes in the pattern of consumption which the United States showed between 1960 and 1967 (Table VI) will be approached by other countries as incomes rise. This would seem to indicate an increase in the consumption of meat and a fall in milk consumption, for instance. But this is too simple a deduction; the American

TABLE VII. *Estimated Per Capita Consumption of Meat Pre-war, 1950–2 and 1959–61, in Selected Countries*
(Kilogrammes per head)

Country	Pre-war*	(ranking)	1950–52	(ranking)	1959–61	(ranking)
Australia	119·2	1	108·9	3	112·6	1
New Zealand	102·4	4	107·8	4	107·6	2
Uruguay	110·1	2	125·1	1	99·8	3
Argentina	106·6	3	114·7	2	96·8	4
United States	69·2	6	82·1	5	94·9	5
Canada	60·1	8	67·0	6	79·0	6
France	55·2	9	56·0	8	73·2	7
United Kingdom	66·5	7	53·7	9	72·4	8
Denmark	69·5	5	56·5	7	66·5	9
Ireland	54·9	10	53·0	10	62·3	10
Germany (Federal Republic)	52·8	11	46·2	12	55·1	11
Sweden	49·0	12	50·4	11	50·0	12
Netherlands	35·8	14	32·1	14	42·9	13
Norway	37·9	13	35·3	13	37·7	14
Yugoslavia	25·6	15	19·8	15	28·1	15
Italy	20·1	16	15·9	16	27·2	16
Greece	19·6	17	11·9	17	23·2	17
Japan	2·2	18	2·4	18	5·3	18

* Average of several pre-war years.

Source: FAO Commodity Bulletin Series No. 40, *The World Meat Economy*.

TABLE VIII. *Per Capita Consumption of Butter in Certain European Countries, 1960–6*

(Kilogrammes per annum)

Country		1960–2	1963–5	1966
France	(a) Consumption	7·7	8·3	8·5
	(b) Price*	1·80	2·0	2·05
United Kingdom	(a)	8·8	8·8	9·0
	(b)	1·00	1·12	1·15
Italy	(a)	1·5	2·0	1·8
	(b)	2·25	2·30	2·38
Denmark	(a)	10·7	10·4	9·8
	(b)	1·4	1·29	1·53
Ireland	(a)	16·3	15·9	15·8
	(b)	1·37	1·42	1·50
Switzerland	(a)	6·7	6·6	6·5
	(b)	2·48	2·63	2·78
Germany (Federal Republic)	(a)	8·7	8·7	8·5
	(b)	1·66	1·85	1·94

*In U.S. dollars per Kilogramme

Source: *Review of the Situation in Europe at the end of 1967*, United Nations. New York 1968.

appetite for dairy products has been diminished by the dissemination of the theory that animal fats are a cause of heart disease; the British, so far, seem unimpressed by the evidence for this. In general, national patterns of consumption show a quite remarkable stability over medium time spans, unless there is a material change in conditions of supply, as happened with the introduction of frozen foods, or the broiler revolution which dramatically lowered the price of poultry.

Table VII shows changes in meat consumption in several countries over a period of twenty-five years. The striking increase of over 25 per cent in the United States and France has not been paralleled elsewhere. The similarity between the ranking of the countries in order of per capita consumption over 25 years is remarkable.

A similar national stability is shown in the consumption of butter (Table VIII). Some countries show evidence of price elasticity of demand, but this is true of both a high price country such as Switzerland and of a low price country such as Denmark. In France (fairly high price) and in the United Kingdom (low price) butter consumption has increased as price has risen. Evidently there is a traditional national habit of eating, or not eating butter, which shows no clear correlation with price or per capita income (Fig. 1).

This is particularly unexpected when we consider that within a single country there are major regional differences in tastes in staple foods. The Welsh, for example, eat 54 per cent more butter and 29 per cent more mutton and lamb than the British average; perhaps they are still close to their pastoral roots. North Country housewives are much given to home baking, and buy 67 per cent more flour than the average; but why should the Scots eat 67 per cent less pork and the Midlanders 47 per cent more pork than the average?

Habit and tradition play so large a part in the determination of consumer demand for food in the medium term that, given that they know for what special market they are producing, and assuming that

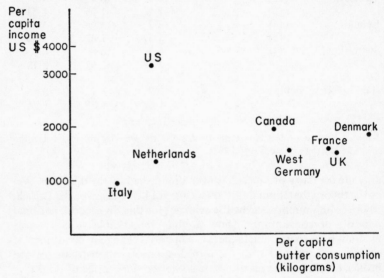

Fig. 1
Per capita income and per capita consumption of butter in certain countries, 1967.

fluctuations in supply from external sources can be regulated, farmers, and governments who increasingly plan agricultural production, may well take conditions of demand as given in all but the longest production periods.

We noted that as income rises a declining proportion of each increment is spent on food. In the United Kingdom in 1965 only cream, poultry, fruit juices and (apparently the height of luxury) frozen peas had income elasticities of demand of more than 0·5. For all the basic foods the income elasticities of quantity purchased, already low in 1955, had fallen. This suggests that in the future the actual quantities of food purchased are not likely significantly to increase except as population increases. A greater proportion of the housewife's money will go to the processors of foods, to packers and freezers, and quality will count for more in her choices.

The modern British or American housewife does not take price into account to any great extent in making her purchases; that is, price elasticities of demand for most foods are below 0·5; only beef, pork and some processed foods have price elasticities of more than 1·0. Producers will, in these circumstances, find that receipts fluctuate inversely with price changes caused by natural fluctuations in supply.[3] Vegetable- and fruit-growers will be most affected by such unforeseen fluctuations. Where own-price elasticities are fairly high, as for beef and pork and some fruits, the danger is that demand will be switched to a substitute food in periods of lower supply and therefore higher prices; such cross elasticities of demand apply as between beef and pork, butter and margarine, and between all-the-year-round fruits such as apples and seasonal fruits. Like own price elasticities, cross elasticities are generally low.

Seasonal Changes in Demand

Even though the elasticity of demand tends to be low in respect of price changes, it does show autonomous shifts; these have little relationship with supply conditions, but much with the weather—salads are favoured when the weather is hot, soups when it is cold—and much with tradition; the peak demand for turkeys in the United Kingdom is at Christmas, but in the United States it is at Thanksgiving Day. It would be a great deal more convenient for the producers if these seasonal peaks could be levelled, and advertising campaigns are launched to induce the consumption of such foods at other times of the year. Where peaks persist, producers must choose whether they will meet peak demand by having much of their plant—turkey houses, glass houses—empty for part of the year, or by diversifying the use of plant in off seasons—for chicken-rearing, say, or for other glasshouse crops such as chrysanthemums—or by storing the finished product till the peak time for consumption, if this is possible. The deep freezing of poultry has made possible a better utilization by producers of plant and labour so that peak demands can be met without a disruption of production programmes and without violent changes in price.

[3] If the price elasticity of demand for a food is 1·0, total receipts remain constant as the quantity sold changes.

If the price elasticity is less than 1·0 total receipts rise as unit price rises and fall as unit price falls; in this case an increase in supply will mean a fall in total receipts.

If price elasticity is more than 1·0, total receipts will fall as unit price rises.

E

Short-term Demand

We may regard as short term the conditions of demand that a producer faces when he actually brings his product to market. The more perishable the product the more important does this short-term aspect of demand become.

If demand for a perishable product is relatively inelastic as it is for, say tomatoes (price elasticity of demand 0·31) the wholesaler and retailer know that price reductions will have to be disproportionately high to clear the market if supplies rapidly increase; a 10 per cent fall in price would induce the customers to buy only 3·1 per cent more tomatoes. If there is a sudden spell of hot weather and tomatoes ripen quickly, there may well be a rise of 30 per cent in the quantity of tomatoes offered for sale; retailers would have to lower their price by 93 per cent to sell all the tomatoes on offer. Retailers may well decide that they can afford to do no such thing; they and wholesalers cannot suddenly expand staff and premises and containers to deal with a large crop at a minute margin over its purchase price. They may therefore decide to buy little more than their usual quantity of tomatoes, and the rest may remain unsold on horticultural holdings; equilibrium will not be reached in such a condition of short-term demand.

A perishable crop with an elasticity of demand greater than unity is a different matter; in this case a rise in quantity offered could cause a disproportionately less fall in price and still clear the market; if price elasticity is 2, then a 30 per cent rise in quantity offered will induce only a 15 per cent fall in price, and total receipts will rise. When retail prices remain sticky in such conditions, as when there is a sudden glut of strawberries, growers demonstrate the fact that the consumer price elasticity of demand is greater than unity by selling the increased crop at less than the current retail price on roadside stalls. In these circumstances middlemen are heavily criticized, but not always justly; they may well have calculated that the extra revenue from the increased sales will not be as great as the increased cost of making those sales; on the other hand, they may have made no such calculations and the growers' charges of inertia may be justified.

In the short term, therefore, the demand at producer level may not bear any discernible relation to the actual or potential demand at retail level. In one sector of the trade in agricultural produce this is a declared policy of British retailers. This is the market for meat, where butchers try to keep retail prices as steady as possible; they assert that consumers do not want to have to balance the relative prices of different meats—beef, lamb, pork—as supplies vary, and so butchers themselves perform a complicated balancing of margins. When beef supplies are scarce and wholesale prices therefore high, butchers do not increase their selling prices proportionately; they take a reduced margin on beef, and a higher margin on pork or lamb. Similarly when wholesale prices of beef fall, butchers do not pass on a proportionate price fall to customers; they may take a higher margin on beef, and less on other meats. When prices of all meats move together, total margins are increased or decreased, and retail price varies disproportionately little. This process may be convenient for the housewife, and presumably for the butcher, but it does remove any influence which retail price elasticities might have on the pattern of production; if price does not vary, price elasticity cannot be discerned.

Wholesale Markets and Price Determination

For a wide range of agricultural products the relationship between retail demand for the final processed food and wholesale demand for the agricultural raw material is tenuous. Wheat prices, for example, in so far as they relate to the wheat content of bread and confectionery, do not move in response to the public's bread-eating propensities; there is a very low price elasticity of demand for bread, and prices of wheat are fixed at wholesale level, prices of flour and bread being derived from this wholesale price, plus many other factors such as wages, costs of packaging and so on in the milling trade, and distribution costs.

The major commodity markets approximate to the conditions of pure competition; there are many buyers and very many sellers, and recognized grades of product, so that, though there may not be the absolute homogeneity of product that is necessary for the conditions for pure competition to be completely realized, variations create smaller but still completely competitive markets within the total market. With modern tele-communications sales can take place virtually simultaneously, thus fulfilling another condition for perfect competition. The British buyer, for instance, can balance offers of grain from Canada, the United States, France, Russia and so on in a matter of minutes. The effects on producers of changes in demand may be cushioned by the intervention of governments or marketing boards, but these agencies themselves are open to the influence of medium-term demand changes on price. The United States Government, for example, can decide next year's cropland adjustment programme for winter wheat in the light of this year's demand and the level of stocks held.

ot Nall wholesale markets function in conditions of perfect competition. Major stock auctions where many livestock dealers regularly buy have a large degree of competition, but at the smaller markets buying is in the hands of local butchers or dealers who, except in conditions of overall scarcity of fatstock, take very good care not to run up prices; a very small increase in supply can lead to a drastic fall in prices. The art of the cattle dealer and livestock fattener is to know when and where to buy and sell and when to keep out of the market altogether.

Because of the spatial separation of markets prices may vary in any one week; for instance, in the week ending October 8, 1969, the average price per hundredweight for light steers (prime beef) varied from 210 shillings at Norwich to 182 shillings at Truro. At some markets the price fell by more than 10 per cent from the previous week; at others there were price rises. Some markets near to large consuming centres regularly return lower prices than some further away, though in general the lowest prices are at the distant rural markets,[4] as location theory would predict.

Perishable products such as fatstock do not lend themselves to distortions of the market by speculative buying: products such as grain, which can be stored, and which are often bought for delivery months ahead, may attract the attention of speculators: their activities force down prices on a falling market, since they tend to sell in fear of further price falls, while on a rising market they add to demand, since they expect further price rises. The pursuit of short-term gains produces de-stabilizing effects: support buying, at times of low prices, has a contrary, stabilizing effect, since the aim here is to hold stocks till demand increases and prices rise.

The smaller the farmer's scale of business and the more precarious his financial position, the more he is at the mercies of the vagaries of the wholesale market. This is particularly true of the producers of store stock (half-grown beasts); this section of the market is hyper-sensitive to changes in demand conditions such as may be caused by seasonal factors such as shortage of grass on fattening farms, or changes in farming practice such as the growth of all arable systems, or by high or low prices for fatstock. Such changes are not movements along a demand schedule but are shifts of the demand schedule to the left. A report[5] on north of England sheep farms, where every autumn the hills must be depopulated of stock, and the lambs and older ewes sold to lowland farms, records a fall

---

[4] *Farmers' Weekly:* price series (weekly).
[5] S. Robson, *Sheep Farming in Northern England 1957–1959*, University of Newcastle, 1961.

of 30 per cent in average prices of ewes between the autumn sales of 1958 and 1959; individual farms recorded falls of as much as 58 per cent. The relevance to hill farmers' profits and plans of the consumer price elasticity of demand for mutton and lamb (0·13) is difficult to discern. If the fall in demand is in fact caused by low prices for finished stock because of an increase in supply (a rise in imports or an increase in home supplies) then the low price elasticity of final demand will be a relevant factor; the normal response of fatteners will be to reduce supply and therefore purchases of stores. Seasonal factors and changes in husbandry methods are not related to final demand.

Other Buyers of Agricultural Produce

Wholesalers, retailers and consumers all buy some agricultural produce direct from the farmer, but increasingly the first buyer of agricultural produce is either a food processor, a retail firm with a large chain of shops, a co-operative, or a statutory marketing board. Commercial firms usually make contracts for one season with producers; this has the advantage of fixing demand for that period, but tends to have the disadvantage that the terms of the contract may not remain the same for consecutive seasons. If there are many competitive buyers the farmer may be able to trade off the offer made by one against that made by another, but the numbers of large firms offering contracts are few and there are very many farmers so that the producer finds himself at a bargaining disadvantage when his contract is due for renewal. It was the activities of the monopsonistic buyers of milk (a few major dairy companies) in terminating and arbitrarily altering from season to season the terms of contracts with milk producers (while safeguarding their own distributive margins) which was one of the features of pre-war milk marketing in Britain which led to the setting up of marketing boards for milk in 1933.

If the farmer sells to a producer co-operative or marketing board he may still not be cushioned from changes in demand—nor, indeed, should he be except in the very short term, since the continued production of unwanted surpluses of commodities is not an economic allocation of resources—but he is more likely to be able to plan his production for any one year without wondering what demand conditions will be when his product is mature, since producers' marketing agencies normally attempt to operate price stabilizing policies.

In some countries certain products, notably dairy products, are bought by government agencies for welfare distribution; milk is the only food so treated in the United Kingdom, though the consumption of some other foods is probably increased by their use in subsidized school lunches. Fifteen per cent of all retail consumption of liquid milk is subsidized and about 3 per cent is distributed free in schools. Measures such as these shift the demand curve to the right. The United States has various schemes of direct food distribution to low-income families, and subsidized food purchases through the food stamp programme. If home production of a certain food is outstripping demand, governments which have guaranteed agricultural prices find these methods of food disposal and subsidization fill more than welfare needs; the current offers of cheap butter by European governments to institutions are not meant primarily to improve the diet of their inmates. Similarly food aid to underdeveloped countries will increase demand and so raise price at each level of supply.

CHAPTER IV

The Supply of Agricultural Products

It is commonly said that agricultural production is carried out under conditions of perfect competition; these conditions are that:

1. there is for any market a very large number of independent producers none of whom produces such a proportion of total output that he is able to influence market price by offering or withholding his product;
2. there is also a large number of similarly independent buyers, none of whom individually is in a position to influence price;
3. the produce in any one market is homogeneous;
4. all buyers and sellers have at any one time full information about the ruling price in the market.

We have seen that there are certain features of the demand for agricultural products which differ from the perfectly competitive norm, but it is in general true to say that for producers the market is competitive; there are in the world millions of farmers, each of whom produces only a very small fraction of total global supplies of any one commodity. In very many cases selling is completely unorganized, and the farmer is a price taker; this is especially true of the less developed countries where farmers sell in competition with one another to merchants in remote villages where the competitive buying conditions of major wholesale commodity markets are absent. In developed countries certain commodities are sold under conditions of if not perfect competition at least a great measure of competition. Such are horticultural products, most of which pass through central markets where price is determined by auction or by bargaining between individual sellers and buyers. Dairy cows, fat-stock sold 'on the hoof' (as opposed to that sold to a wholesaler or butcher by private contract with payment at previously agreed rates) store cattle and sheep, grain sold from farms to merchants, are all sold in conditions which approximate to those of perfect competition. One has only to compare agricultural marketing in Britain, with its very many auction markets, produce markets and wholesalers, and thousands of independent producers with, for example,

71

the motor industry, with four main producers and a network of controlled retail outlets with fixed or 'recommended' prices to see that, despite some imperfections in some sectors of agricultural marketing, agriculture is still a highly even if not perfectly competitive industry.

In conditions of competition between suppliers, price is determined by the reactions of producers to prevailing demand; in Fig. 1 the demand schedule is fairly inelastic which, as we have seen, is characteristic of consumer demand for most foods (say it is for

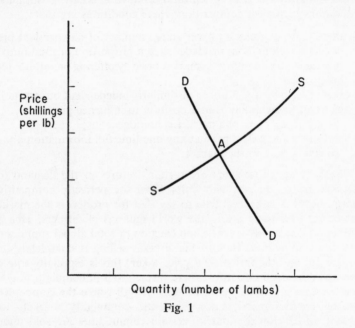

Price (shillings per lb)

Quantity (number of lambs)

Fig. 1

lamb). Sheep farmers have, in the spring, a certain number of lambs which mature at different rates according to date of birth, breed and feeding. Lambs are offered at successive dates through the late spring, summer and autumn. If demand is steady price will depend on supply; one hundred lambs ready in May may fetch 4 shillings a pound dressed carcase weight, but in the same market five hundred lambs ready in July may fetch only 2 shillings and 9 pence a pound. If farmers are willing to sell at the price so arrived at the market will be cleared. If butchers are willing to buy more lambs than are on offer on any one day, price will move upward along the demand schedule till equilibrium is reached at a higher price; if farmers offer more lambs than butchers want on market day, price will move downward along the demand schedule till the market is cleared.

When supply and demand are in equilibrium each seller will cover his total costs, including normal profit; at this point also marginal cost and marginal revenue will be equal, that is the amount each farmer receives for the last lamb which he is willing to sell at the prevailing price equals the cost to him of rearing and bringing to market that last lamb. If price were to be established above point A, more farmers would come forward with lambs till the price fell again which is indeed what happens, since a farmer with lambs to sell will watch the market and send off a batch of lambs when 'trade is good'. If price were to be established below point A farmers would, if possible, keep lambs on the farm in the hopes that smaller supplies would mean a rise in price.

Products which show marked seasonal variations in supply will, in unregulated markets, also show variations in price; even the most intensive methods of production have not entirely eliminated the hen's propensity to lay more eggs in the spring than in winter, and egg prices fall as the seasonal supply rises. Such vegetables as broccoli show marked seasonal fluctuations in supply and therefore in price. There is a natural increase in milk production in May when grass is at its best; beef is most plentiful in autumn as beasts finish the summer fattening period. If there is no interference with the inter-play of supply and demand these products will show the typical counter movements of price and supply of the model of pure competition.

This model does in fact reproduce conditions in some agricultural markets, such as those just described, at single points in time or over very short time periods. But there are imperfections in agricultural markets and peculiarities in the supply of agricultural products which make the model of only limited use.

Farmers as Non-maximizers

The model of price determination in conditions of perfect competition relates to the actions of maximizers—producers who cease production at the point at which marginal revenue equals marginal cost. But not all farmers are maximizers, at least not all the time or for all products. Studies of the behaviour of milk producers[1] have shown that farmers over the age of fifty tend not to increase milk production even when relative costs and revenues are such that an

[1] Milk Marketing Board, *Changes in Milk Output 1963 to 1967*, Milk Marketing Board, 1968.

increase would be profitable; young farmers are more likely to be maximizers. The farmer who spends two days a week at hunt meets or gossiping in the auction mart or involving himself in parish affairs may maximize his *satisfactions*; he does not necessarily maximize his *profit*. What proportion of farmers may thus be non-maximizers depends on the terms of trade between agriculture and the other sectors of the economy; when the terms of trade move against agriculture a much higher proportion of farmers are likely to be maximizers.

Similarly farmers may be non-maximizers by expanding output or expenditure beyond the point at which marginal revenue begins to fall below marginal cost. It is comparatively easy to do this in farming because of the operation of the Law of Diminishing Returns. Cattle cake may be fed to cows long after the point at which increasing increments of cake cause the cows to produce the equivalent value of extra milk; beasts may be over-fattened and so make a less price per hundredweight than if they had been sold earlier. The latest combine or forage harvester or silage tower may be bought not because it will increase revenue or cut costs by more than its purchase price but because the man next door has one. There are fashions in farming as well as in consumption goods. Nevertheless farmers in general over the whole of their farming life do not behave noticeably more irrationally than other sections of the community; the fact that some farmers are not profit maximizers would not be worth comment if it were not sometimes noted, as if it were peculiar to agriculture, that producers sometimes prefer leisure to maximum profit. Non-maximization is in any industry an imperfection in competition.

Perverse Response of Supply to Price

There are two types of perverse response of supply to price. First, supply may rise in response to price rises up to a certain point, and thereafter, while price continues to rise, supply may decline (Fig. 2). This response must seem irrational if the price of the commodity is the only changing determinant of supply considered; in fact it will often happen that other factors—the price of inputs in the production process, the prices or cost of production of other agricultural commodities which might be produced as alternatives, the opportunity costs of capital and labour—will change and, given that demand is relatively price inelastic, it will be rational for producers to decrease production of the first commodity and to increase that of others, or to take jobs out of agriculture. In certain circumstances it will be rational for farmers to reduce *sales* of crops when prices rise even though they do not reduce production; if these farmers are normally under-fed they may be able in times of high prices to eat as much as they want and still cover necessary expenditure by sales of smaller quantities of produce. In all such cases 'backward sloping' supply curves are not perverse; they seem so only if we forget that in the model of pure competition the only stimulus to which supply responds is price, and the assumption is that other things remain unchanged.[2]

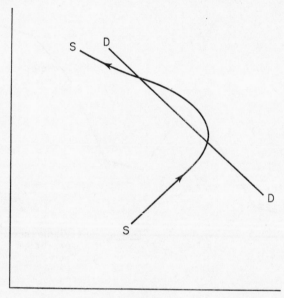

Fig. 2

Secondly, supply may not fall in response to falling price. This reaction is typical of agricultural production; one well-documented case is that of milk production in England and Wales in the years 1955 to 1963. In these eight years the average price paid by the Milk Marketing Board to producers fell by 10 per cent; costs of labour rose by 46 per cent (measured by the rise in the minimum wage for agricultural workers) while the cost of compound dairy cakes (the other chief variable cost in milk production) initially rose, then fell, then rose again to its 1955 level. Meanwhile the farmer's cost of living had risen by 28 per cent.[3]

[2] A relevant case study is E. Dean, *The Supply Responses of African Farmers*, North Holland, 1968.
[3] Milk Marketing Board, *Thirty-Sixth Annual Report*.

The moment of price and output as plotted in Fig. 3 seems per-verse. In this case there was no lack of comment by farmers on the increasing disparity between price, costs and output; in 1963 a working party set up by the National Farmers' Union reported[4] that a scheme for the payment of a bonus to producers who did not

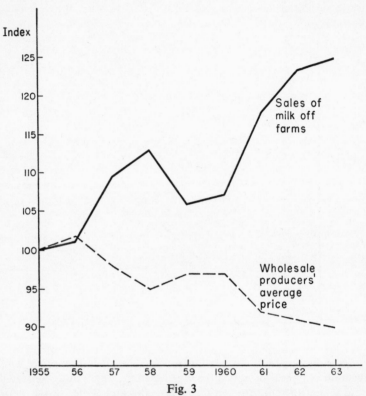

Fig. 3

Perverse response of supply to price Type 2: rising supply with falling price (Price and supply of milk, England and Wales, 1955–63).

Source: Annual Reports. Milk Marketing Board of England and Wales

exceed a certain agreed amount of output was desirable to limit the increasing floods of milk which, given that demand was unlikely to increase, were reducing the price of milk to farmers to what were felt to be ruinously low levels. The scheme was overwhelmingly rejected by the milk industry. Milk output has continued to rise in

[4] Boden Committee: *Report*, NFU, 1963.

the 1960s, though at a slower rate than in the 1950s. Price per gallon has risen, but in the year ending March 1969 it was only 7 per cent above the 1955 price, while labour costs had doubled, feed costs had risen 13 per cent and the cost of living index had risen by 59 per cent.

In considering this type of apparent perversity of response to price movement several peculiarities of the supply of agricultural products will come to light.

Changing Technology and its Effect on Supply

The equilibrium position illustrated in Fig. 1 is that of a static situation; it depicts market conditions when demand and supply in total are already exogenously determined, and what is in question is how much of the commodity will in fact be sold at the price which is acceptable to both producers and consumers in any one market at any one time. But the supply conditions for agricultural commodities are constantly changing as technology changes. The effect of such a change in technology is to shift the supply curve to the right (Fig. 4). In the post-war years striking technical advances have occurred in most sectors of agriculture. Yields per hectare of maize

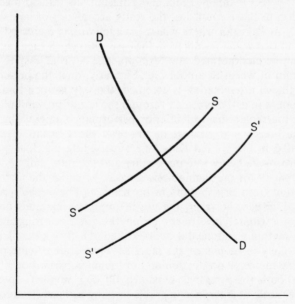

Fig. 4
The effect of improvements in technology on supply.

have doubled in the United States between 1954 and 1967, through the use of improved strains of plant and more fertilizer; the acreage of maize harvested for grain has fallen to an average of five-sixths of its 1954 level during the mid-1960s, but the maize grain crop has increased by nearly 50 per cent; unit prices have declined by 10 per cent on average from the mid-1950s to the mid-1960s. In the United Kingdom yields of barley per hectare have increased by almost 50 per cent from the early 1950s to the late 1960s, through the use of improved strains, more fertilizer and better harvesting techniques. Specialized corn growing has increased, and with it economies of scale in the use of machinery. Consequently there has been a marked shift to the right in the supply curve for barley; between 1950 and the late 1960s the area sown to barley has increased by 300 per cent, total crop has increased by 400 per cent, while price to the producer (including deficiency payments) after a sharp rise at the beginning of the 1950s has subsequently slightly declined.

Where technical improvements come from research establishments and from agriculture's ancillary industries the threshold of acceptance of the new means of production may be very low. In the two harvest seasons 1968 and 1969 for instance, the use of improved strains of cereal plants in India and Pakistan has transformed food production in those countries; the ready acceptance of new strains, especially in Pakistan where wheat production has increased by 50 per cent in two years, results from the ease with which such improvements can be incorporated into farm practice—it is as easy to sow a good strain of wheat as a poor one. Similarly, once the principle of using artificial insemination is accepted, the way is open to a rapid improvement in cattle breeding through the use of proven bulls, and through the replacement of inferior performance animals by those of better breeds and strains; in this way the Friesian breed has proliferated in the United Kingdom, superseding the dual purpose Shorthorn by its better milking quality and the pure dairy Ayrshire by its capacity for producing beef carcases. Much of the increase in milk output from British dairy farms has been due to the spread of this breed. When, however, the use of improved methods depends on a major capital investment or on the total rearrangement of working methods and mental outlook then the threshold of acceptance is likely to be higher, the more so when scale of enterprise is small. The intensive production and optimum conservation of grass have for both these reasons remained till now minority methods; the bigger scale of enterprise in arable farming has largely accounted for the more rapid acceptance of technical improvements in that sector.

Technological changes have not, in general, increased productivity in dairying as much as in arable farming; but the late 1950s and early 1960s saw the adoption of two simple labour saving techniques, the use of a milking 'parlour' in which the cows come to the milker instead of his having to go to each cow individually in her place in the shed, and the practice of letting the cows pull their own long fodder from a silage clamp instead of the workers having to cut the fodder and carry it to the cows. The productivity of labour at the farmstead doubled by these methods; unit costs in milk production fell, labour being the highest input cost after feeding-stuffs. So the larger farms were able to maintain output with diminishing labour costs, and the smaller farms, where labour is that of the family and therefore irreducible except in conditions of extreme pressure on profit margins, were able to increase output without a proportionate increase in costs. At the two extremes the largest farms whose opportunity costs of milk production were highest turned to arable farming, and the very smallest farms whose supply price could not come down to that of the whole industry gave up milk production. The increased output of the remaining producers appears as a 'perverse' response to price.

The supply curve for the whole industry is not, in this type of case, the sum of similar cost curves for all firms, but an amalgam of differing cost curves, some producers being in equilibrium with normal profits, others making residual profits and others making losses. The position of the supply curve will be determined by the proportion of producers in each category and by the state of technological development of the industry. Where, as in the dairying industry and, indeed, in much of the agriculture of the developed world the proportion of output accounted for by producers making normal or residual profits is much higher than that accounted for by producers making losses, the supply curve will move steadily to the right; where even normal agricultural profits (which we saw in Chapter II were less than those in the manufacturing industry) are not made, the supply curve, in the absence of technological improvement, will move to the left, as seems to be the case at the present time with the British sheep industry, where prices have been static and profits declining for years, and, in the absence of major technological change, total numbers of sheep are now falling.

Joint Products

These are products which are produced inseparably as the result of one process of animal or crop production, but which are marketed separately. Examples are lambs, wool and ewe mutton; milk, calves and cow beef; grain and straw. The relative value of the joint products varies; from one sheep we may get in her lifetime eight lambs worth £56, six fleeces of wool worth £6 and finally a mutton carcase worth £4. The sheep farmer's production plans naturally concentrate on the number and quality of the lamb crop; if wool prices rise he will be pleased to get a little extra profit, but in costing his sheep enterprise he will think in terms of the probable price of fat lamb and not the probable price of wool. (In New Zealand his priorities might be reversed; the value of the wool crop may exceed that of the fat lamb crop.)

In the short term there is nothing that the farmer can do to increase or reduce the relative proportions of such joint products. If wool prices fall disastrously he will still have to sell his year's production of wool, unless he is able to forego his income from wool altogether and to store the fleeces in the hope of a price rise. If prices of lamb are such as to make sheep rearing profitable, the wool market will continue to attract supplies even if wool prices are on a falling trend. Similarly, if milk production is profitable and beef production is not, supplies of young calves will continue to be offered at markets, and, if supplies greatly outnumber the demand for calves for rearing, the price of all but the very best beef calves may fall to very low depths indeed.

In the longer term the farmer may well be able to alter the proportions of joint products by changing his breeding policy; he may get better calves with more attraction for beef breeders by using a beef bull to cross with his milk cows; he may lessen the amount of straw that has to be dealt with after harvest by growing short-strawed varieties of grain. In the very long term, plant and animal geneticists may be able to alter the proportions of joint products even further. At any given point of sale, however, there will often be apparently perverse responses to price trends in agricultural markets where joint products are sold.

Complementary Products

The difference between joint and complementary products is that the former are inescapably produced together and the latter are produced in conjunction as a matter of choice.

Commercial (as opposed to subsistence) agriculture in the tropics is notable for the predominance of monoculture; this is especially true of plantation agriculture and tree crops, where biological difficulties in the long-term production of one crop only do not arise. Complementary products largely appear in temperate agricultures where the monoculture of any crop except grass and trees has hitherto brought some difficulties.

Such products as wheat, roots, grass and livestock may be produced on a farm as part of a planned rotation of cropping, the object of which is to maintain soil fertility and to avoid the proliferation of soil-borne diseases and of weeds. Such rotations were for centuries characteristic of the farming of European countries; in recent decades they have been to an increasing extent abandoned as the need to achieve economies of scale in the use of machinery and the benefits of specialization by the labour force have replaced long-term considerations in farm planning. The practice of monoculture of cereals has not yet been carried out for long enough for anyone to decide whether the use of chemical fertilizers and pesticides will permanently be able to supersede the production of complementary products; there has been, however, some recent emphasis in Great Britain on the growing of crops such as beans and oats to break the monoculture of wheat and barley. The traditional break crops—roots and grass—involve the keeping of some livestock to utilize the fodder so grown; a very careful costing of the capital investment the variable costs and the total returns to the farm from each possible form of complementary product must be made in every case; sheep, for instance, need little capital equipment but they do need a shepherd; dairy cows need a considerable capital investment in buildings and plant, and are themselves rather costly articles to buy.

A simple 'gross margin' costing of such enterprises is liable to give a misleading impression of total costs and benefits to the farm as a whole; benefits in the form of increased yields of other crops will not appear in such costings, nor will such benefits become apparent in the short term. The farmer who produces complementary products may seem, therefore, at a single point of time, not to be maximizing profits.

Inflexibilities of Factors of Production

In Chapter II we noted that choice of farming enterprise may be limited by the inflexibility of one or more of the factors of production. The farmer in a favoured area of good climate and soil has a wide choice of products; in New Zealand, for example, he may grow grass to feed cows and sheep, or grain, or fruit, with better yields per hectare than his European rivals. Within even a small country such as Britain the fertile soils of East Anglia and parts of the south-west give a much wider choice of production systems than do the heavy boulder clays of much of the north-western hill areas; this advantage, combined with a generally sufficient but not usually

F

excessive rainfall makes farming in the low-lying southern and eastern counties much more flexible in response to changes in demand than that of the north and far west. The north-western dairy farmer may continue to produce milk in spite of falling price because he has no alternative; he cannot grow grain on his steep hillsides and with his sixty inches of rain a year. Between 1964 and 1967 there was a fall of 18·6 per cent in the numbers of registered milk producers in England and Wales. The largest falls were in the east and south-east regions, respectively 28·1 and 29·5 per cent. These are areas where the choice of farming systems is not restricted by soil or climate. In the same period the number of producers in the north-west and mid-west regions fell by only 15·6 per cent and 14·9 per cent respectively; the figures accurately reflect the comparative range of alternatives.

Size of farm may also limit choice of systems; the man who has two hundred hectares in England may grow grain or feed beef cattle or keep dairy cows, or mix his enterprises; the man with twenty hectares cannot make enough profit per hectare in anything but intensive dairy farming, pigs or poultry, or horticulture to leave him a net income large enough to live on. A tobacco and livestock farm in the Kentucky bluegrass country may have a net farm income from 25 hectares as high as that of a 250 hectare wheat farm in the Southern Plains; but the Kentucky farmer would not be able to survive if he put his small acreage into wheat. Availability of labour may also be a constraint on possible changes in the pattern of production. On the one hand a shortage of labour will lead to adoption of simple farming systems, which will be less intensive in land use as well as in the use of labour (for instance, beef grazing instead of dairying or monoculture instead of mixed cropping). On the other hand on many family farms labour is a fixed input, and systems intensive in labour use, and therefore in general more intensive in land use, will be adopted; specialist grassland farming with rotational grazing and cutting and much use of fertilizer, and pedigree livestock breeding with emphasis on individual high performance animals are two examples. A fall in the price of animal products may only induce the livestock farmer who uses family labour to increase output; he thereby spreads his fixed costs over a higher total output, and as he does not make actual payments for the labour of himself and his sons he receives a higher net income.

A major constraint on choice of systems is that of the availability and cost of capital; a major change of production policy, say from all dairying to some corn growing, may be out of the question if no financial capital is available for the necessary machinery and corn drier. Once capital is tied up in a set of buildings and plant suitable for only one productive process, it may equally prove impossible for the farmer to change his plans even though the profitability of that particular product may decline; for example an automated pipeline feeding system for pigs will not be of any use for other livestock if pigs become unprofitable.

Traditionally British and much Western European farming has relied on the mixing of enterprises to avoid the pitfalls of total inflexibility of production which may result from commitment of land and fixed capital to one product. If cattle rearing was less profitable it was easy to keep a sow or two in the cow sheds, or to grow a few acres of potatoes or keep a few dozen breeding ewes. The need for greater productivity of labour and so for greater complexity of capital inputs has made this kind of quick change of policy almost impossible. Once committed to one line of production the farmer tends to increase output when price falls; the apparently perverse response of British dairy farming to the price falls of the 1950s and early 1960s was in part caused by capital inflexibilities of this kind.

Agricultural Supply in a Period of General Depression

If the prices of *all* agricultural products fall the reactions of farmers are inevitably unlike those of industrialists. Suppose there is a slump in the motor-car industry; at first, factories which make cars will be put on short time—the available work will be shared out among the existing work force. If it becomes apparent that trade is not going to recover some factories may be shut down, and men and plant will be idle. Such action will maintain the unit price of the smaller number of cars manufactured. Farmers cannot carry out a comparable operation. If cows and sheep and crops are all unprofitable it is not possible to shut down farms entirely; as long as the land is there it must grow something, even if that something is only the indifferent grass that grows on its own when once farmed land is left uncultivated. Farmers, being self-employed, cannot receive unemployment relief until such time as trade recovers; they have the simple choice between increasing production and so mitigating the fall in incomes by taking a less unit profit on a bigger output, or going bankrupt.

During the depression of the early 1930s, for example, wheat prices in Britain fell to 50 per cent of their level in the mid-1920s; the acreage of wheat grown declined by only 24 per cent. Cattle numbers, after a fall in the late 1920s, rose again to more than their previous total, while sheep numbers increased though prices fell. This does not mean that cattle and sheep were highly profitable, though their profitability relative to that of grain increased for a time. The forces of inflexibility of factor inputs made the maintainance of output the only alternative to complete bankruptcy.

Similarly in these years of depression the output of the New Zealand dairy industry increased by 48 per cent; this was partly because comparative costs fell more in dairying than in other livestock sectors because of the high proportion of labour in total costs (wages fell by 16 per cent) and partly because, though all prices fell, those of sheep and wool fell more steeply than those of dairy products. In this case the physical factors of production were flexible and the composition of total output changed, but in spite of the fall in all prices total output was maintained.

Countries which depend on the exports of agricultural produce may suffer a drastic fall in total income in such a time of economic depression; the United States, Australia and New Zealand all saw the value of their agricultural production decline between 1929 and 1931; the fall in the United States is estimated to have been over 50 per cent, and in New Zealand over 42 per cent. Measures to restrict supply are not easily accepted by an industry with thousands of producers in every country; consequently in a time of general trade depression agricultural production tends to be maintained, while industrial production falls.

Production Periods and Inflexibility of Supply

If a farmer is growing corn he makes his production plans for one year in the autumn of the previous year, when he sows winter wheat. His current year's crop is by then harvested, but it is not until months later that he will be able to tell what the average selling price of corn for the crop as a whole will be (immediately after harvest prices are at their lowest level, for most farmers want ready cash and offer all or part of their crop at the same time). If prices are initially low, and remain so during the winter, the farmer may decide not to sow as much spring corn as he had originally planned. If this reaction to low prices is widespread the supply of corn will fall in the next harvest year, prices will then rise and probably production will rise again in the next production period.

Grain crops, with their growth period of only a few months and with a choice of sowing dates have one of the more flexible supply responses to price changes. Most horticultural crops are similarly price responsive, but other products tend to show inflexibility of supply because of their longer production periods. Breeding cattle, for example, take two years from birth to calving; beef cattle take eighteen months to three years, according to type and feeding, from birth to beef. To this must be added the gestation period of nine months that must elapse between the farmer's decision to breed a beef or dairy type calf, and the birth of the calf. Within this total period of two to three years production is not entirely inflexible; if a dairy calf is bred it may be sold at birth as a 'bobby' calf (made into meat pies) if at that time the outlook for a future expansion of the dairy herd is gloomy. A half-grown beast may not be bred from, but slaughtered herself at about breeding age. Between the initial decision to breed a dairy calf and maturity there are thus two opportunities for production plans to change. Similarly if milk is less profitable than beef the older cows will not be bred from again but will be sold as cow beef.

It will be noticed that this type of change is all in the direction of reducing supply; it is not so easy to increase the supply of milk or cattle in the short term. Something can be done by feeding more concentrates to the existing herd, but the response of cattle to concentrate feeding above a certain level is doubtful, and doubtfully economic. So an increase in milk supply is mainly brought about by a decision to increase the dairy herd by retaining old cows and breeding more calves; from the latter decision to maturity will take two and a half to three years. Similarly, though a short-term increase in the beef supply is possible, and indeed a short-term decrease is also possible if dual-purpose animals such as Friesians which were originally intended for beef are bred from instead, any long-term increase will depend on plans made more than two years before.

The greatest inflexibility is shown by tree crops; a rubber tree takes seven years to come to maturity, and its productive life is twenty to thirty years. Once a rubber plantation is established it is difficult to reduce production very much—(it may be reduced to some extent by not tapping some trees in some years but the planter will need *some* income, and will almost certainly have to market some of his product, however low the price)—unless trees are felled, and this is an irreversible diminution of supply which it is not easy for the planter to accept; so with other tree products such as coffee, cocoa, fruits and timber. The last is a particularly inflexible form of production; the man who plants a stand of Douglas fir knows that he or his successors must wait about forty years (in British climatic conditions) for the trees to reach maturity; the thinnings will have some small value, but the sawn timber crop must either be left to mature or sold at a price that will not recompense him for many years' use of the land. Hardwood timber takes even longer to mature in temperate climates, and commercial planting of hardwoods is very rare.

Because of this inflexibility of production period, most tree crops have very low price elasticities of supply; rubber trees planted in the period of high prices during and after the Korean War could continue to produce rubber till into the 1980s. The peak price for rubber was reached in 1951, and by 1966 it had fallen by over 50 per cent; meanwhile, because of the long production period, world output of natural rubber had increased by over 40 per cent. Coffee has shown similar price inelasticity of supply. During the 1930s the burning of stocks of coffee was a notorious example of maladjustment of supply and demand; by 1940 supply had declined, but high prices after the Second World War induced an increase in plantings, so that by 1966 production was higher than in the immediate post-war years, while prices had fallen to about 60 per cent of their 1952 level.

Such inflexibilities of supply cause considerable instability in the incomes of producers of tree crops, many of whom are exporters of tropical agricultural products. One recent example of this is world trade in cocoa. All cocoa-producing countries increased plantings in the 1950s; by 1966 world production had increased to 60 per cent above the level of the early 1950s, and unit prices had fallen to less than 50 per cent of their 1958 peaks. This proved disastrous for the newly independent state of Ghana which is dependent on cocoa for 85 per cent of its foreign exchange earnings.

Perishable Products

It is the nature of all agricultural products to be consumable and so more or less quickly perishable. This is most obvious in the case of horticultural products, but though other crops may be stored they need special conditions of storage which may make it impossible to deal with a large surplus.

Fig. 1 illustrated the supply schedule of a commodity which may be offered in varying amounts according to producers' reactions to consumer demand. Highly perishable products will not show such a response to demand price; strawberries, for example, are saleable for only a few days, and if the market is over-supplied much of the crop will be unsaleable. We may illustrate price determination for a highly perishable product by a diagram such as Fig. 5; price elasticity of demand from strawberry-eaters is high when prices are low (dd) but, as we saw in Chapter III, elasticity of demand from the wholesalers may, for a variety of good or bad reasons, be less elastic (d'd'). In the middle weeks of July the supply of strawberries will be totally inelastic (S); all the crop will be ready and must be sold. If the trade is geared to collecting and selling a quantity OQ of strawberries, a sudden increase in supply because of, say, unusually good weather will put on the market more fruit than will be sold (OQ''). Whole-salers' demand may move from point A to point B, far enough to the right to take the quantity OQ', but not far enough to take the quantity OQ''. The quantity $Q'Q''$ will be unsold though consumers' elasticity and demand to the right of B' may be high; in these circumstances growers must leave their crop to rot, or, according to their temperament, take it to throw at their Minister of Agriculture.

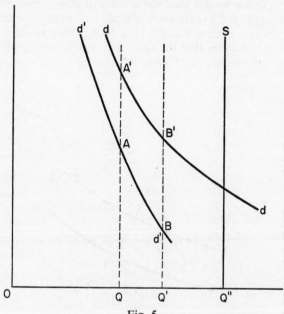

Fig. 5
Price determination for a perishable product

The supply of some livestock products is, from the producers' viewpoint, equally inelastic at the point of maturity; young stock such as lambs and calves which are reared on summer pasture often have to be sold before the winter to farmers who preserve fodder for winter keep; the upland rearers sell such 'store' stock at special autumn sales, and there the effect of an unusually large supply, perhaps because there was a heavy lamb crop, is to force prices down to levels which may leave no profit on the rearers' year's production. Demand from farmers who fatten lambs and cattle is price elastic, and it is unusual for a willing seller not to find a sale at some price, but the price so obtained may leave the seller no profit on the beasts sold.

Flexibility of Supply and Cycles of Production

Some agricultural products take a comparatively short time to mature; their response to price changes is not at all like that either of slowly maturing tree crops or of some perishable products, but shows a characteristic cyclical movement.

Suppose that a market gardener decides to grow a crop of lettuce; his first sowings of the season will be ready in June, and on marketing them he perhaps decides that the price he is getting is not as high as normal; he concludes that the market is over-supplied, and accordingly he reduces his later sowings. His individual supply curve

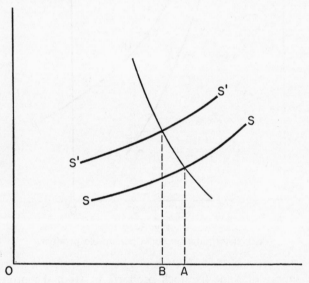

Fig. 6
Price determination with variable supply.

shifts to the left, and if his views are shared by other lettuce-growers, the total supply curve for lettuce will shift to the left also.

If lettuce-growers have made a correct assessment of the supply situation, and if demand remains steady, price will rise, and equilibrium in the market will be reached at a higher price than the original price. In Fig. 6, the first price will be OA, and after a movement in the supply curve from *ss* to *s's'* the new price reached will be *OB*.

Perhaps, however, lettuce-growers have been too pessimistic; when supply is reduced there may remain some unsatisfied demand, and a larger quantity of lettuce might have been sold. A sharp price rise will be an indication of such a maladjustment, and a sharp price rise will tempt some growers to increase sowings again, and perhaps other growers to begin lettuce production. If all or most producers react in the same way, demand remaining fairly inelastic, price will fall, production plans will be amended accordingly, and the cycle will begin all over again.

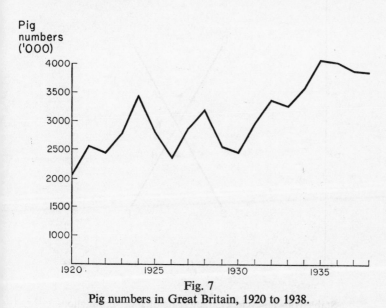

Fig. 7
Pig numbers in Great Britain, 1920 to 1938.

There are many agricultural products for which this sequence of events is normal; vegetables show a distinct cyclical tendency to two-year cycles, higher production and lower prices in year one being followed by lower production and consequently higher prices in year two, and so on. Pigs are notoriously subject to cyclical swings of production; the chart (Fig. 7) of pig production in Great Britain shows that pig numbers used to fluctuate in a cycle of about three years between peaks and troughs. Before the Second World War, the length of cycle was influenced by the production period of pigs (which was longer than it now is because today's improved breeds of pig mature more quickly than formerly, and today's taste in bacon and pork demands a lighter pig) and also by the price of feed grains. Pig numbers fluctuated around a fairly stable long-term equilibrium, and could be shown on a diagram such as Fig. 8 as a stable cobweb-cycle. To produce such a stable cobweb both demand and supply curves must be similarly elastic; if they are equally elastic, oscillations round the point of equilibrium can persist indefinitely.

We have seen that demand for agricultural products, at any rate from the final consumer, is probably fairly inelastic in high-income

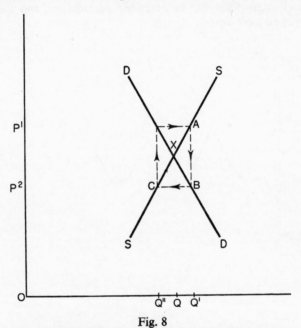

Fig. 8
Stable cobweb-cycle, characteristic of short-production-period crops and fast-maturing livestock.

Equilibrium between supply and demand would occur at X. A movement of supply from its initial position by an increase from OQ to OQ' will cause a movement along the supply curve from X to A. But for this quantity of produce (say pigs) buyers are prepared only to pay OP, so that demand price falls to B. This price is unacceptable to many producers, who revise their plans and reduce production. to OQ''. At the consequent point C on the supply curve there are not enough pigs on offer to satisfy demand; prices again rise, production is increased and the cycle begins again. Changes in technology and shifts of the demand curve may alter the parameters without eliminating the cyclical tendency.

countries. A cycle of supply would then produce a divergent cobweb as in Fig. 9. Pig producers are more willing to expand pig numbers quickly than are consumers to eat more pork. This cyclical progress cannot continue indefinitely; production will not be expanded to the point at which price falls to zero, and the cycle will eventually return to the form of Fig. 8, though there will be painful moments for pig-producers in the process, and some will leave the industry.

In Britain guaranteed prices for pigs have not ironed out the cyclical movements of pig numbers; even a built-in formula for taking into account the level of feed prices when fixing the guaranteed price did not stabilize the pig population. Evidently the prolificacy and fast-maturing qualities of the pig have an inherent tendency to induce cycles of production, and this has for some years now been

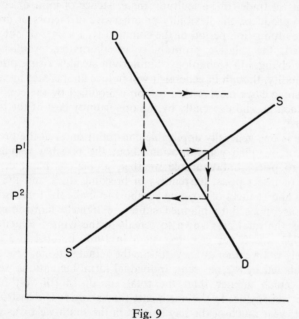

Fig. 9

Divergent cobweb-cycle characteristic of increasing supply with inelastic demand.

taken into account by making the guaranteed price vary according to the number of pigs entering the market. If numbers rise above a certain desirable maximum, or fall below a stated minimum, the price is lowered or raised with the aim of inducing a counter-movement in pig numbers. This 'middle band' of permissible pig numbers is itself altered from time to time. The whole exercise has now become so extremely complex that few farmers understand it; if the aim of the exercise is to influence supply through price such complexities are self-defeating. Whatever the reason, the pig cycle continues.

Uncertainty and the Decision-making Process

Cycles of production arise in response to three factors, the present price of the product, its relationship to that in the previous period and expectations about the direction of future price changes. A price that falls steadily over time will not give rise to cycles; whether it induces the response of a fall in production for the commodity in question depends on the various limiting factors already discussed— the terms of trade for agriculture, the existence of joint or complementary products, the flexibility or otherwise of factors of production, the production period of the commodity, whether or not it can be stored, the relative profitability of alternative products and relevant changes in technology. Similarly a steadily rising price for a commodity, though in general it will induce an increase in output, will in some cases meet with a response modified by the conditions of production, and especially by the opportunity cost of the factors employed.

There is one generally applicable constraint on even the broadest and most qualified generalization about the possible response of supply to price; unfavourable weather, animal or plant diseases, attacks of insect pests, barrenness of breeding-stock and the other changes and chances of farming combine to make the forecasting of actual, as opposed to planned supply, extremely hazardous. For instance, the total area sown to cereals in the United Kingdom in June 1968 was 2 per cent less than in 1967, but because of the extremely wet weather at harvest time the actual national production of cereals fell by 8·2 per cent. Individual farm fluctuations were, of course, much greater than the total; in the north-west harvest weather was idyllic; in the north-east the harvest was disastrous. In the same year much of the hay harvest in the south-west was ruined by floods, and freak hail storms stripped vegetable crops in several places. All this happened in a small country of generally equable climate; the nation-wide crop failures of countries which depend on the monsoon and of continental areas which experience severe droughts have in recent years dramatically altered the world conditions of demand and supply for cereals from season to season.

The natural hazards of farming mean that the individual producer knows in advance neither what his own production will be nor how much of the product will be offered on maturity by his fellow farmers; his response to price is thus decided in conditions of uncertainty which he can do little to change. Market forecasts can only say what acreage of a crop or what numbers of animals are in the pipeline; what will be offered for sale is not accurately predictable. Farmers in food-importing countries face also the hazards of sudden influxes of imports when world production of commodities rises. In such circumstances the natural tendency will be for farming to be undertaken in ways that minimize risk; response to rises in market price is likely to be sluggish, response to falls in market price is likely to be exaggerated.

The physical conditions of uncertainty in agriculture, together with the fact that farmers individually are price takers, means that any measures which introduce an element of certainty into the marketing of farm products are likely to have a disproportionate influence on supply. Such measures may be control of prices or control of quantity produced or marketed, and they must now be considered.

METHODS OF CONTROLLING AGRICULTURAL SUPPLY

The Effect of Guaranteed Prices on Supply

A price guarantee for an agricultural product may take one of several forms; it may be a simple open-ended guarantee of a certain price for any quantity which is put on the market, or it may be a guarantee applicable only to a certain previously decided output. It may apply to all grades of a product, or only to certain quality grades. In an importing country the guaranteed price may take the form of a minimum price for imports, or it may take the form of a 'deficiency' payment which is an added payment to producers bringing their total receipts up from the price of imports to an agreed level. Governments or marketing boards may put a floor in the market by support buying when price falls to a pre-determined level, and by the holding of buffer stocks. The methods of financing guaranteed prices show an equal variety. These matters must be dealt with in detail in Chapter VII.

However the guaranteed price is financed and administered, its effect will be to induce a greater supply at any given price level than would be induced by the same price determined by market price mechanisms only, for market price carries no guarantee of continuity. This is well illustrated by the relative prices and areas sown o wheat and barley in Great Britain in the 1930s. The area sown to +wheat was about 770,000 hectares in the early 1920s; by 1931, in the depths of the depression, it had fallen to 500,000 hectares. A deficiency payment for wheat was introduced in 1932, and the area sown increased again till by 1938 it had regained the level of the early 1920s. Meanwhile the area sown to barley fell from 410,000 hectares in 1932 to 328,000 hectares in 1938; for some years the total return to barley was higher than that to wheat, but whereas the price of barley was the open market price, that of wheat had a guarantee.

There can be no doubt that one of the reasons for the steady expansion of milk production in the United Kingdom since the war has been the existence of a guaranteed price for a fixed ('standard') quantity of liquid milk. This has fluctuated from the price announced in the *Annual Review and Determination of Guarantees* by as much as 9·4 per cent (in 1962) but, with subsequent measures for the partial control of imports of dairy products, it puts an effective floor to any fall in price induced by an increase in production. Earlier in this chapter we noted the apparently perverse response of British milk producers to a continuous fall in the price of milk, measured in 'real' terms, that is, in relation to the cost of inputs and the purchasing power of the pound. To the factors which contributed to this response, we must now add a guaranteed price, announced in advance, changed very little from year to year, and paid by monthly settlements which greatly reduce the need for large borrowings of working capital by the milk producer. A clearly understood guaranteed price, fixed at a level which eliminates the marginal producer but allows an acceptable profit to the efficient producer, and so administered as to remove the necessity for long waiting periods for payment, is probably the best way of inducing sufficient supply of any product without calling forth unmanageable surpluses or burdening the non-agricultural part of the community with large transfer payments. In an uncertain world the farmer will do much to obtain a measure of certainty.

A price guarantee may not be easily understood, or it may be determined in such a way that the producer does not actually know in advance what price he will get, or the relationship of price guarantee to market price may be so determined as to place an undue emphasis on the latter; then the results of introducing a guarantee may not turn out to be those intended by the supporting authority. For example, the United Kingdom Government in 1965 announced that an expansion of beef supplies from the home herd was desirable[5] 'to the full extent of the technical possibilities', in the five years 1965 to 1970. An undertaking that there would be no reduction in the guaranteed price for beef or in the beef-cow subsidy in that period

[5] *The National Plan*, 1965.

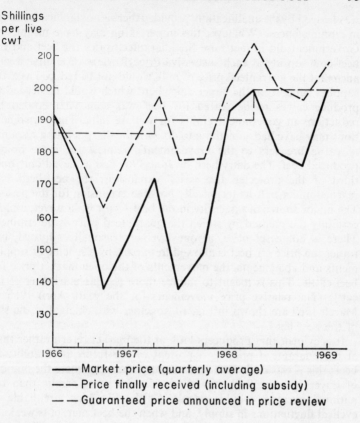

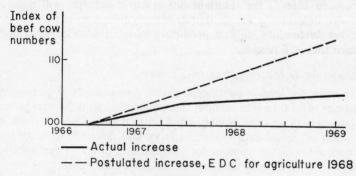

Fig. 10

Market price: guaranteed price for fat cattle and beef-cow numbers, 1966–8, UK.

was hedged by the qualification 'provided there is no significant change in circumstances'. Whatever this undertaking may have meant, the Government did in fact raise the guaranteed price for beef and the beef-cow subsidy at each successive Price Review. A similar assurance that the guaranteed price of milk would not be reduced as extra supplies came from the larger dairy herd which would be needed to produce calves to be reared for beef was somewhat eroded by reductions in government grants for welfare milk. These qualifications may have had something to do with the disappointing response of cattle breeders to the Government's request for more home-produced beef. The dairy herd by June 1969 had achieved only one-third of the projected five years' expansion; the beef herd had reached under half its technically possible expansion for the period. The major source of insecurity in the beef sector is, however, almost certainly the method by which the guaranteed price is determined. There is not a set price, at one level or seasonally adjusted, but rather the price for beef is allowed to mirror, by a scheme of supplements and abatements, the movements of the open-market price for beef cattle. This is meant to induce more regular marketing of fat cattle. The relative price movements for the years April 1966 to March 1969 are shown in Fig. 10, together with changes in the size of the beef herd.

It is evident that producers look at the market return rather than at the guaranteed price as a portent of the future profitability of beef; this is especially true in the smaller markets where the number of buyers present fluctuates and prices are more erratic than the national averages would suggest. Cattle, like pigs, are liable to cyclical fluctuations in supply, and when the beef market is weak, as it was in 1966–7, the resultant downturn in supplies will not be avoided unless the guaranteed price entirely eliminates unpredictable market fluctuations, so that producers know in advance what unit return they will receive.

Reasons for Introducing Price Guarantees

In fixing the level of guaranteed prices, governments or marketing agencies must take into account the many constraints on changes in supply which we have already considered if they wish to attain a position of equilibrium between supply and demand. In addition, governments may have aims for guaranteeing prices to agricultural producers, which limit the range of choice of price levels.

First, they may wish for strategic reasons to keep up a level of production which requires a higher than optimal use of the country's resources in agriculture; it may be better to grow at home some food which might be bought more cheaply abroad if there is any danger of insufficient food supplies in time of war, of disruption of transport from other countries, or of the aggravation of balance of payments difficulties by the need to pay for very large food imports. Guaranteed prices set at levels which do not induce unmanageable surpluses are probably the best way of maintaining in being an agricultural sector large enough to provide an efficient base for any expansion which may be needed in the future.

Secondly, governments may wish to stabilize the incomes of farmers which, if determined solely by the market forces of supply and demand and by the hazards of weather and biological factors, tend to fluctuate widely from season to season. Where the agricultural sector is large the effect of such fluctuations will be to induce undesirable cycles in the country's economy, and stabilization of farm incomes may be one means of maintaining steady growth.

Thirdly, governments may wish to raise the incomes of farmers so that they do not lag too much behind those of other sectors as a country becomes more highly industrialized. If the disparity in productivity between the agricultural sector and the rest of the economy is very great, a price level which enables all the resources currently employed in agriculture to remain there will be injurious to the country's total economy; if, on the other hand, prices are set at a level which compels the rapid withdrawal of labour and capital from agriculture, there may be much hardship to rural populations, either because the sudden transfer of agricultural families to the towns reduces the population of rural areas so much that it is impossible to keep up essential services for those who do remain, or because the 'stickiness' of factors causes farmers to hang on to their farms when incomes fall to very low levels; in fact, where there is rapid withdrawal from agriculture, as in some hill areas of European countries and in some of the problem areas of the United States, both factors will operate, and rural depressed areas will be formed.

These three reasons for guaranteeing agricultural prices are not to be dismissed out of hand because they interfere with the free operation of market forces or produce temporarily higher levels of supply than purely economic considerations would dictate. Temporary maladjustments of supply to demand may be preferable on welfare grounds to the creation of a depressed class within a country, and the long time period in which agriculture adapts to price changes may make some kind of guarantee with its consequent higher-than-optimal level of production inevitable. The desire of governments to win the rural vote is a less legitimate reason for guaranteeing prices,

G

and for raising the level of such guarantees in election years. British farmers may now be so few in number that this consideration no longer operates with their governments; the 1966 Price Review was not particularly generous in spite of the imminent election. In Europe, however, and in parts of the United States, the farm vote is still powerful, and it may prove more difficult to undo policies and levels of price support which have resulted in the late 1960s in burdensome surpluses of produce.

Price Guarantees and Consumer Price Levels

A guaranteed price will, over a period of several seasons, raise returns to producers above the level which would obtain in conditions of free competition or, in the world of trade in agricultural commodities today, of competition subsidized by governments other than their own; consumer prices will therefore also probably rise above the possible minimum level, though the amount by which they will do so depends on the method of financing the price guarantee to farmers. Direct exchequer payments to farmers to supplement market prices will limit or even eliminate consumer price rises; in this case a price guarantee for any agricultural product is a transfer payment to farmers from the rest of the economy, and also a transfer payment from those who pay taxes to those who do not. This has to a large extent been the British system of price support. If the higher price to farmers is simply passed on to the consumer, there is a transfer payment from all consumers to producers; in this process the middlemen also benefit if they add a percentage margin to the farm-gate price. Tariffs on imported produce, import levies which raise import prices to a minimum level, intervention prices which operate at wholesale levels, all raise consumer prices.

Where subsidy is paid direct to the farmer, total consumer demand is likely to be higher than it is where tariffs, levies, or support buying at wholesale level is the chosen method of price support. The higher the price elasticity of demand, the less will be consumption as price rises. For many commodities in developed countries, as we saw in Chapter III, price elasticity of demand is so low that there will be little difference between the levels of consumption with either type of price guarantee. For meat, many fruits and vegetables, and cream, *price* elasticities are more than unity, and in these cases total consumption will fall if the introduction of a price guarantee raises consumer price. As *income* elasticities of demand are higher for these products than for others, the implications of choice of method of price support must also be considered by governments in relation to the income distribution of their countries. This involves not only welfare implications but estimates of the probable aggregate of demand and therefore of the appropriate supply of the products in question. For grains, which are inputs in livestock production, price guarantee by deficiency payments will reduce the need for higher prices for the end product: high farm-gate prices will escalate costs in livestock production.

The control of the volume of supply by the adjustment of price, however it is carried out, is therefore a very tricky operation. Slightly too high a guaranteed price will probably produce surpluses of the subsidized commodities; the 400,000 tons of butter at present stored in the EEC are evidence of such a miscalculation. Too low a price may unduly, and in the short run irreversibly, reduce supply as happened with rice in Burma and Thailand and with beef in Argentina, when price was reduced too much by export taxes. It is consequently tempting for governments or marketing authorities to attempt to by-pass these difficulties by introducing direct physical controls on the volume of supply, or controls on the levels of inputs into agriculture.

Physical Control of Supply

The simplest and oldest method of physical control of supply is the storage of produce in times of surplus for use in times of scarcity; for thousands of years it was normal farm practice to make cheese and butter from the summer surplus of milk, to store grain, to salt dry meat, to store roots in clamps of soil, and some of these practices continue today; processing, however, as opposed to simple storage, is now usually carried out by specialist manufacturers, who have themselves to make a profit from the process and who therefore may not be able to provide manufacturing capacity to deal with the whole of a seasonal surplus. For this reason producers' co-operatives and marketing boards (see Chapter V) have invested in manufacturing plant, financing this by levies on members' sales of produce. As long as such enterprises cover variable costs and depreciation on capital, it will pay farmers' organizations to finance them rather than to throw away part of the seasonal surplus of production. The financing of processing plant is less risky when the capacity can be used for several products in rotation; vegetable and fruit canners, for instance, have an extended season, and can turn their attention to citrus fruits and other products in the winter; dairies have a short and sometimes unmanageable surplus in the late spring and early summer.

Processing as a measure of supply control applies only to seasonal surpluses; where total annual supply outstrips demand other measures of control have been attempted.

Quotas

In a number of countries the supply of certain commodities is limited by the imposition of quotas which apply either to the overall production of a commodity or to the amounts which individuals are allowed to produce or market. If demand for the commodities subject to quota is inelastic, total receipts from the market will not fall as much as will total supply, and it may be possible to reach an equilibrium of supply and demand at a somewhat higher price than formerly without the introduction of measures of price support. If demand has a price elasticity greater than unity the imposition of a quota will entail some price support if farmers' incomes are not to suffer a disproportionate fall.

Global Quotas

The British Government has been able to operate a global quota for milk for many years in the form of a guaranteed price for a 'standard' quantity of liquid milk. Supplies above this standard quantity realize only the lower prices for milk for manufacture. Producers are not paid according to the actual realization price of their individual supplies of milk, but all receipts for milk, for whatever purpose it is sold, are pooled, and the average price so arrived at becomes the effective guaranteed price for milk. This has fallen below the guaranteed price for the standard quantity in every year since 1957, by amounts varying between 2·7 per cent and 9·0 per cent of the standard quantity price, as supplies have varied from year to year. Such a global quota system does not achieve a precise adjustment of supply to demand in the short term; what its long-term effects are likely to be will depend on the actual price level relative to the total conditions of supply.

A similar global quota for eggs operated for some years in Britain; the guaranteed price was determined in relation to an indicator price which was the price the Egg Marketing Board would expect to receive from an adequate but not excessive supply of eggs. If supplies rose to the point at which market-price fell well below indicator-price, actual returns to producers fell also; there was thus a built-in incentive to restrain supply increases. In 1964 a 'standard quantity' quota scheme was also introduced for cereals; in this case there is no marketing-board to distribute total receipts among producers, and individual deficiency payments are made to growers by the Government at the end of the sales year, according to the relationship between market receipts and the 'target' price set for cereals at the beginning of the season. The 'middle band' limitations on total pig numbers to which the price guarantee applies is a similar scheme.

Global quotas of this kind were in operation in the Netherlands for sugar and in Luxembourg for all agricultural products before the adoption of the EEC common agricultural policy. They have been criticized by producers because they do not limit total supplies as long as some of the more efficient producers are able to operate profitably with the falling prices that accompany an increase in total supply beyond the quota limits. From the point of view of consumers, however, global quotas are beneficial in that they allow the benefits of increased productivity to be passed on in the form of lower prices. Governments like them because they effectively limit the extent of exchequer support for the commodities under quota. To be effective in maintaining producer-price such quota schemes must be accompanied by both some form of price guarantee and a limitation of imports; producers will not willingly accept restriction of home production if the beneficiaries are foreign exporters.

Individual Quotas

If a government wishes the supply of any agricultural commodity to be fixed, the imposition of quotas on individual producers would seem to provide the most effective way of doing so. Unless marketing is through one or a few well-defined organizations it is, however, in practice very difficult to know exactly what each producer is selling. Acreage quotas, or quotas based on the head of livestock on a farm, may approximate to sales, but there will be seasonal and individual variations which such methods cannot estimate in advance; moreover producers may thwart the intentions of governments who seek to limit supply by acreage quotas by concentrating production on their better land and intensifying production on their alloted acreages. This has been common in the United States, where acreage quotas have at different times been imposed for maize (corn), wheat, cotton, peanuts, potatoes and rice. Acreage quotas have, therefore, to be effective, often to be reinforced by price differentials for sales above certain quantities by each producer.

Transferable Quotas

Individual quotas imposed at one point in time may simply ossify the structure of agriculture if there is no provision for their proportions to be altered at intervals. The sale of quotas between producers is the most effective way of securing this necessary alteration; the less successful or those about to retire may sell their quotas to others whose costs of production are lower and who are willing to expand production. Such a transferable quota scheme has operated successfully for hops in the United Kingdom, for sugar-beet in France and in a few other cases.

Effectiveness of Quotas

For individual commodities which are in over-supply, the imposition of quotas may be an effective way of achieving supply adjustment, since farmers can concentrate on the production of alternative commodities which are not subject to control: the United Kingdom hops and sugar-beet quotas are examples. Where there is general over-supply this becomes impossible, and if quotas are extended to major products or to a wide range of products either farm incomes decline or the cost of agricultural price support becomes intolerable to the rest of the community. The smaller the proportion of the national product that agriculture contributes the easier will be such continued support, and the less harm will accrue to the whole economy from supply restrictions.

Where there is world over-supply of a commodity the attraction of international quota schemes is obvious; the co-operation demanded of governments and individuals in working such schemes is, however, almost super-human, since to a government faced with supply of a commodity in excess of its quota, the temptation to sell for any price at all rather than to destroy crops or buy them for storage is almost irresistible. The two principal schemes of this kind, those for sugar and coffee, both broke down, the one because of political developments in a major producing country (Cuba), the other because of lack of co-operation by some member countries (see pp. 133–35).

Control of Supply by Means of the Inputs into Agriculture

In most countries measures designed to induce an outflow of *labour* from agriculture will have little effect on total agricultural output; in less-developed countries this will be because labour tends to be under-employed in the sense that the same output can be obtained with a smaller but more effectively used labour force, while in developed countries the substitution of capital for labour will allow the agricultural labour force to fall to very low levels indeed without any effect on total supply, though the pattern of output may change to some extent from labour-intensive to capital-intensive products; thus livestock may be reduced in favour of highly mechanized arable cropping. Measures such as assisted farm amalgamations which reduce the agricultural labour force tend to maintain output and to improve the incomes of those who remain in agriculture.

Policies which directly attempt to retain labour in agriculture are

rare; the various rural development policies of European governments and the similar programmes of the United States Department
of Agriculture attempt to improve the rural infrastructure and thus
to make rural life tolerable to those farmers and their families who
remain in remote areas rather than positively to keep labour in these
areas. The special headage payments and other grants to hill farmers
in the United Kingdom have, as agricultural output has increased,
probably become simple social payments to the farm labour force in
these areas; they were not introduced with that object, however,
but to keep up the contribution of the hill areas to total supplies of
meat and of breeding-stock.

There have been many programmes of subsidy for *capital* inputs
into agriculture both with the aim of increasing output and also in
order to give cost advantages to farmers when the low price of their
outputs or their limited scale of enterprise would not give them an
acceptable income and allow them to pay market-rates of interest
on investment. These programmes may run concurrently with
measures for the withdrawal of labour, since an increase in capital
inputs may be labour-saving; this is true of investment in machinery
and fixed capital. Subsidies to inputs such as fertilizer, fuel or
feeding-stuffs will not save labour; they may, in fact, increase labour
needs, and will certainly raise output. Subsidized credit may have
either a labour-saving or an output-increasing effect according to the
relative prices of inputs and output; it may also tend to push up the
price of agricultural inputs. Subsidizing capital inputs when agriculture prices are kept at low levels is one way of re-allocating consumer
incomes; taxpayers' outlays may keep down prices to all consumers.

Land is by far the easiest input to control; it is, within narrow
limits, fixed in quantity; it has, except in areas of urban development, low opportunity costs; the policing of measures for the control
of land use is comparatively easy.

When governments want to increase output they may undertake
schemes of land reclamation, or by such policies as grants for ploughing and reseeding of grassland, drainage or fertilizer use they may
seek to improve land which is already in cultivation. In conditions
of over-supply, the withdrawal of land, either from specific crops or
from cultivation altogether will seem an effective method of reducing
supply. It was noted above that acreage quotas for individual
crops are not necessarily effective, unless they are reinforced
by sales quotas, or unless they apply to commodities of which
total output in a given country is small. Programmes for total
retirement of land from farming have been operated for some time
in the United States, whose land resources are much larger in com-

parison with national needs for agricultural produce than are those of most European countries. The first programmes, begun in the 1950s, had the usual drawback of being to some extent offset by diversion of over-supply to other commodities; farmers also tended to withdraw their poorest land and to increase production on the rest. In the 1960s the aim of land-retirement schemes has been to convert land use to forestry, recreation and other non-agricultural uses. One disadvantage of land-retirement schemes is that it is usually the least productive land which is offered for retirement from agriculture, so that the effect on total supply is negligible. Unless land-retirement is part of an effective scheme of rural development in which whole areas are considered as economic and social units and alternative work provided for those displaced from agriculture by the withdrawal of land, so that the inducement to give up farming altogether is strong, their effect on supply is likely to be insufficient to outweigh the social costs of their implementation (see Chapter VII).

CHAPTER V

Agricultural Marketing

In the last two chapters we have been discussing the activities of many buyers and many sellers of agricultural commodities; both operate in small units and none can individually influence price. The producer and the ultimate buyer very rarely meet. The producer-retailer of milk is still common in parts of Great Britain, and in most rural areas elsewhere; the market-gardener who has a roadside stall or takes his own produce to a local market is still found, but the proportion of the consumer market so supplied must be very small indeed. The inhabitants of large conurbations could not possibly be supplied with food by direct selling by producers; for instance, milk from farms in the extreme north-west of England goes daily to the London market, and loads of beef are regularly taken in refrigerated lorries from the north-east of Scotland to London; individual producers could not afford the time or the specialized equipment which would enable them to reach these distant markets. This is not a recent development; the old drove roads on which cattle once trekked to London in charge of specialist drovers are remnants of a much earlier division of labour in the agricultural marketing process. It is sometimes alleged by economists and by farmers that other parts of the food marketing chain are similar relics of a former age.

We may ask of the marketing of any particular agricultural product:

1. How does the market function?
2. Are all the existing functions of the market necessary?
3. Are they efficient?
4. Does the producer receive a fair share of the price paid by the consumer?

I. TYPES OF FOOD MARKETING

Auction Markets

The most usual method of marketing agricultural produce has for very many years been the collective market; produce from a very

105

large number of scattered farms is assembled in one place, and buyers come from a distance to bid for what is on offer. Such a market has every appearance of perfect competition, and it might be expected to provide the optimal service both to producers and to consumers; for producers the auction market should be the source of information on current trends in supply and demand, as reflected in prices; for the consumer the competition of sellers and buyers in the auction should guarantee that the true price of the produce is arrived at and that the benefit of falls in price due to increases in supply is received, as well as the dis-benefits of price rises.

For several reasons the auction system does not, however, function perfectly. First, there need be only a small change in supply to produce a quite disproportionate change in price; this is particularly noticeable at the smaller markets where the few buyers are very quickly aware of the amount of produce forward, and can hold back their bidding if supplies are ample. In this case the last sellers of produce may well receive much less than the national average price for their stock or produce once demand is satisfied. Where buyers are few compared with sellers, demand is usually fairly inelastic. Secondly, when this disadvantage of smaller auctions is overcome by the use of a few large central auctions, such as Covent Garden in London for horticultural produce and Smithfield for meat, the physical movement of produce into and out of one small and congested central area may greatly add to marketing costs. Third, the system of grading livestock 'on the hoof' at fatstock auctions is an inexact process which may leave both buyer and seller dissatisfied. The seller may, if he is not too distant from his farm, refuse to accept the liveweight grading allotted to his stock and take his animals home in the hope of a better result next week, or elsewhere; the buyer does not really know from grading on the hoof just what sort of carcase he is going to get, and the variety of consumer preference is such that for some retail markets an animal in an inferior grade is in fact the better buy. Fourth, for horticultural produce the time taken from grower to consumer is likely to be lengthened by the need to take produce into and out of auctions, so that the consumer gets stale and often overhandled produce.

The inadequacies of the auction system have caused some economists, agricultural producers and distributors to advocate a change to a system of selling produce by more direct links between farmers and consumers. It is, however, noteworthy that the two Royal Commissions[1] which investigated the distribution of horticultural produce and of meat in Britain in recent years were both fairly well

[1] Committee on Horticultural Marketing, *Report*, Cmnd 61, HMSO, 1957;

satisfied with the workings of the present, mainly auction, system. The United States National Commission on Food Marketing[2] also pointed out the difficulty of price determination in the absence of openly competitive markets. Though the percentage of livestock sold by auction has somewhat declined in Great Britain there are still more than 60 per cent of sales of cattle and sheep so made, and about 20 per cent of sales of pigs. In the United States, where the terminal markets have declined in popularity as the development of large beef feedlots has encouraged direct sales, the present tendency is for markets to turn to auction selling from commission sales to packers simply because auctions are more openly competitive and therefore popular with sellers. The social function of the auction sale also has some, unquantifiable, effect in maintaining its popularity.

Many of the disadvantages of the auction system could be eliminated by farmers themselves if they were to adopt the long-established Dutch system of 'Veilings', that is, the withdrawal of produce from sale once the price has fallen to a pre-determined floor. This applies to horticultural produce, which can be disposed of to charitable institutions or in the last resort destroyed; it would not apply so easily to cattle. Finance for the payment of at least the floor-price to all producers comes from producers themselves by a levy on sales. This system substitutes one form of imperfect competition for another, but Dutch experience does not suggest that the consumer suffers thereby; the more stable prices help to reduce cyclical swings of production and therefore encourage more rational behaviour by producers and in the wholesale and retail trades.

Sales by Private Treaty. The marketing of cereals is the major agricultural market in which sales by private treaty predominate; cereals are bought on the farm mainly by merchants who bargain directly with the producer and sell again to millers, maltsters, brewers and feed-compounders, or in exporting countries to grain-shippers. The second-stage buyers are few, but because the first-stage buyers are many there is a fairly high degree of competition in the grain merchanting business, and no indication that excess profits arise at this stage. Transport costs limit the second-stage markets, which are in any case characterized by a high degree of concentration (there are, for instance, four major flour-millers and eight major feed-compounders in Britain); but there are also still a large number of small concerns which offer alternative outlets to the farmer, and

Committee of Inquiry into Fatstock and Carcase Meat Marketing and Distribution, *Report* Cmnd 2282, HMSO, 1964.

[2] *Food from Farmer to Consumer*, US Government Printing Office, 1966.

flour-milling and business feed-compounding are highly competitive and have low profit margins. The livestock farmer benefits from this competitiveness, and the compounders seek to escape its effects in various ways discussed below.

Much private selling of cattle is done 'on the hoof' on farms, especially in the United States where the development of large feed-lots has encouraged the practice, 70 per cent of their output being sold in this way; it is worth while for sellers of large numbers of stock to become proficient in marketing, bargaining with buyers not only over price but over such conditions of sale as transport and shrinkage allowances. The small seller neither has the specialist knowledge of this side of the trade nor will he find that competing buyers are willing to visit his farm. His alternative to the auction is to sell 'deadweight and grade' to a wholesaler; the Fatstock Marketing Corporation was set up by the National Farmers' Unions of Great Britain in 1954 to provide such a wholesaling service. It now has about 20 per cent of the market for fatstock, mainly pigs; that the method of sale whereby animals go straight from farm to slaughterhouse at a pre-arranged price has not become more popular may be due to its unsociability, but the complexities of the dead-weight grading system which often make the pre-announced price apparently bear no relationship to the price actually received is probably the major cause. There is a peculiar irritation in the telephone call which announces that some of the animals sent off to the wholesaler have been 'rejected for subsidy', and the rider that the seller can go to view the bodies only adds insult to injury. There may in fact be little possibility of arguing with the government grader at the auction market, but at least the animals may live to grade another day.

Contract Selling

The revolution in retailing of food which has been brought about by the growth of chains of outlets which need regular supplies of graded products, has led to an increase in sales of farm produce by contract either to retailers direct, to wholesalers who themselves contract with retailers, or to food processors. Sales of fruit and vegetables for canning or freezing are made entirely by contract, and contract sales of soft, stone and citrus fruits, of eggs, poultry and pigs are common.

The benefits of contract selling are obvious. The farmer who sells in this way eliminates one major source of uncertainty in his calculations, since he knows in advance what price he is going to get and what quantity he can sell at that price (this benefit being less important, of course, where prices are guaranteed in any case by government agencies). He may also get advantageous terms for capital borrowing from the contracting processor, from whom he will be able to obtain specialist advice, and to whom he can leave marketing problems while he concentrates on the technical aspects of production. By specializing on one product he may obtain economies of scale which would be out of his reach if he were to mix his enterprises in order to minimise market risks.

The processors or retailers have, for their part, the advantages of an assured supply at agreed prices (thus eliminating the price rises which accompany a shortfall in production when many buyers compete for produce); by specification of quality and grade they can ensure that they get a standard product amenable to pre-packing for the convenience of shoppers. The consumer should benefit by the elimination of many links in the chain of distribution which ought to cheapen the final product, and which certainly make it more attractive and more reliable.

Difficulties arise, however, for the farmer, when the processor or distributor takes advantage of the producer's commitment to one or a few products in order to tighten margins and in other ways to alter contract terms; (there are, for instance, contract terms for the rearing of broiler chickens which leave the rearer with all the risks of loss from disease or unthrifty chicks with no compensating increase in profit if the chicks do extra well). The wise farmer will commit only part of his equipment to contract production, though by so doing he may forego the benefits of increased scale.

Where a large part of the output of any agricultural product is the subject of contractual arrangements, there may be difficulties for those producers who, from choice, or because they are distant from possible contract outlets, or because their scale of enterprise is too small to attract contract buyers, have to sell their produce on the open market. Their costs of production may be higher than those of the contract producers, and where the latter predominate the concentration of production into fewer specialized units may eliminate the smaller producers. It will clearly pay contractors to deal with as few producers as possible, as long as the latter do not become non-competing oligopolists, since they can thus greatly reduce distributive costs. In production processes which lend themselves to intensification and economies of scale (poultry, eggs, pigs) the reduction in the numbers of producers as contract buying develops may cause problems of adjustment.

The types of contract so far discussed create backward linkages from retailing or food processing to farming; there are also forward linked contracts made largely by feeding-stuff manufacturers, for instance in broiler production, pig breeding or fattening, egg production or the fattening of beef animals in feedlots. The contracting firms usually supply some of the capital equipment, or provide the feed on credit, and in some cases tie the producer to purchase their own brand of feeding-stuff. There are also looser schemes operated by such firms and trading co-operatives in which they merely act as intermediaries between, for example, pig breeders and fatteners. Yet other forward linkages exist between hatcheries and broiler producers or egg producers. The advantages of these contracts to the farmer are largely in access to capital, and to the contractor in guaranteed outlets for his own produce.

Vertical Integration

Vertical integration exists where one firm owns or completely controls several stages of production of a commodity and where at each stage there is produced a commodity which can itself be independently marketed; in agriculture it occurs chiefly in those sections of the industry which also have much contract selling. The United States broiler industry is a notable example of a vertically integrated industry, all stages of broiler production from hatcheries through breeding farms and chick fatteners to wholesale (and sometimes retail) outlets being in some cases under the control of a single enterprise. In such cases the 'farmer' is in fact little more than a paid employee, though he will be paid for his output rather than for this time. When the whole of a production process is vertically integrated there should be an advantage to the firm in that the profits which, in a non-integrated organization, would at each stage go to one of a series of producers, go after integration to the same firm; this should make it possible for the price of the end-product to be lower than might occur otherwise—a relatively unprofitable stage may be carried by the others, whereas if each stage were independent, each would have to make some minimum profit. Whether this will happen does not depend on the degree of integration but on the share of the market which the integrating firm controls and on the ease of entry into the industry. Broilers, for example, demand little in the way of capital equipment and practically no land. There were in 1965 in the United States over 200 broiler processors, of which four controlled 18 per cent of the market; economies of integration and of scale of production have in fact accrued to the consumer, for while United States retail prices have risen as a whole by 24 per cent between 1955 and 1967, the price of broilers has fallen by over 40 per cent. In the United Kingdom, on the other hand, the degree of concentration in broiler processing is such that two firms control 50 per cent of the market, a further 25 per cent being controlled by three other firms. It is no longer possible to enter this industry without the investment of a great deal of capital and a great deal of specialist knowledge, and there is obvious danger both to contracting farmers and to consumers in so high a degree of concentration in a mode of agricultural production which is largely independent of the use of land, so that vertical integration can be combined with considerable market power.

The Efficiency of Agricultural Marketing

In the types of marketing of agricultural produce so far discussed, the farmer has been in all cases a price taker; he may 'negotiate' a contract, but in fact he knows that if he does not accept the contract terms some other farmer will. If he refuses the contract he can take what prices are offered in the auctions or by wholesalers, but in no case can he control price. The final consumer is in a similar position; the collective preferences of consumers do, of course, influence supply, as witness the difficulty the non-conformers find in buying anything but steam-baked sliced bread in English village shops, where the shopkeepers must meet majority demand. They also influence price, so that frying-steak costs twice as much per pound as shin of beef, supply being limited and demand being price inelastic up to this point. Individually, however, neither producers nor consumers can be other than price takers, and naturally both suspect that somewhere in the distributive chain there are persons concerned to see that the margin between the price the one receives and the price the other pays shall be as wide as possible.

Farmers, housewives and economists sometimes seem to think that all that is required to reduce distributive margins is for a large degree of competition, measured in numbers of those engaged, to exist in the wholesale and retail trades. The competitive auction-market remains popular with farmers, and in Britain it took the disastrous years of the early 1930s to induce farmers to abandon their attachment to competitive outlets and to combine in marketing schemes. To the housewife a street full of different shops may seem to offer genuine competition, but it is in France, where small retailers account for four-fifths of all food sold, that distributive margins are high, and it is in the overlapping, rather than competing, small food shops of English country towns that we see in operation a policy of minimum risk—turnover is restricted and prices are kept up. Equally the distributive dairies take the government-fixed maximum price of milk as a fixed price; (there is, however, some price competition among producer-retailers in some local areas). The presence or absence of competition does not seem to be the determinant of the size of margins in distribution, and is not, therefore, a meaningful measure of distributive efficiency. A more useful comparison is provided by the size of the distributive margins in each sector of food distribution as compared with those in other sectors, and the changes in margins over time both absolutely and in relation to the changes in the cost of inputs.

The Size of Distributive Margins

No meaningful comparisons can be made between the unit margins in food distribution and in that of non-perishable goods; for the latter, furniture or electrical goods for example, unit margins at retail level are high because of the large amount of capital which must be invested in stock and the slow rate of turnover. If, however, the margin is expressed as a percentage of turnover, the figures for some types of food retailing approach those for all retail trade but in general are lower (Table I). Profit is, of course, much lower than

TABLE I *Retail Margins in Food Distribution in the United Kingdom, 1961*

	Gross margin as percentage of turnover
All retail trade	24·9
Grocery and provision dealers	16·0
Other food retailers	24·2
Butchers	22·2
Greengrocers	20·9

Source: Census of Distribution, 1961, Pt. 14, Table I, HMSO, 1964.

the percentage price mark-up; United States figures suggest that profits in food retailing and processing are certainly not higher than the average for the economy at large which in manufacturing were largely between 11 or 12 per cent (Table II). It is noticeable that the profits in retailing declined from their peak in 1950, as new firms entered the supermarket industry and the windfall profits of the pioneer food chains were reduced by competition.

The distributive margin varies from one product to another, and is not always calculable in comparable ways. Milk, for example, reaches the housewife in a comparatively unprocessed state; it is, however, taken from farm to consumer in a short space of time, and the elaborate arrangements for transport from farm to dairy, from collecting dairy to distributing dairy, and, after heat treatment and bottling, to the consumer's doorstep, account for the fairly high costs of distribution. The Milk Marketing Board for England and Wales publishes each year details of distribution costs, and Table III is assembled from these figures.

TABLE II. *Profits after Income Taxes of Leading US Food Processors and Food Chains, 1950–65*

| Year | Profits as percentage of net worth | |
	Food processors	Retail food chains
1950	11·5	17·9
1952	8·2	10·7
1954	8·9	13·9
1956	10·3	15·5
1958	10·1	15·2
1960	10·3	13·0
1962	9·9	11·5
1964	11·3	12·5
1965	—	12·5

Source: Table 5, *Food from Farmer to Consumer:* Report of The National Commission on Food Marketing, Washington, 1966.

We see that the total distributive margin for milk was 36·5 per cent of the retail price (maximum permitted price for pasteurized milk). The total margin was made up of a wholesale margin which was one-tenth of the total and a retail margin of nine-tenths; the latter includes cost of heat treatment and bottling and dairy delivery from house to house. The retail margin has widened; in 1955 it was

TABLE III. *Changes in Distributive Margins for Milk in England and Wales, 1955 to 1969 (years ending March 31)*

Year	(a) Board's gross selling price	(b) Marketing and transport allowances	(c) Retail margin	(d) Retail price	(c) as percentage of (d)
		Pence per gallon			
1955	40·53	3·49	13·11	53·64	24·0
1959	45·89	4·13	16·44	62·33	26·2
1964	46·20	3·50	20·52	66·72	32·2
1969	55·87	3·32	27·14	83·01	32·7

Source: *Annual Report and Accounts*, 1969 MMB, Thames Ditton, 1969.

H

only 24 per cent of retail price, and it has been suggested that the cost of milk deliveries could be greatly reduced by alternate day deliveries; it has been pointed out that Britain is unique in having such a doorstep service daily. These suggestions have been very coldly received by farmers who foresee a reduction in milk consumption if the milkman ceases his daily round, and experience with a six-day delivery scheme has recently shown that some of the expected savings do not materialize (the roundsman having to make extra trips to his van to refill his carrier with double deliveries to each house).[3]

TABLE IV. *Distribution Costs of Fresh Milk, United States, 1964*

| | Half gallon (cents) | |
	In stores	Home delivery
Retail price	47·7	52·8
Retailing	7·3	—
Wholesaling, transportation other distribution	7·5	20·8
Processing	9·8	8·9
Assembly	1·4	1·4
Farm value	21·7	21·7

Source: *Food from Farmer to Consumer*, Washington, 1966.

Costs of retailing liquid milk in the United States are given in Table IV for comparison; the margin for milk delivered to the consumer was 59 per cent of the retail price, higher than the British figure; even for milk sold in stores it was 55 per cent. The British housewife's daily home delivery service is cheaper because of the difference in United States and British wage rates. In Denmark the distributive 'spread' is intermediate and accounts for 45 per cent of the retail price; in Russia where 70 per cent of milk is sold loose, the retail margin was in 1965 only 6 per cent of retail price.

Milk is a particularly well-documented product because of the organized nature of its marketing in most countries. Distributive margins for other foods are not so easily ascertained, but in the United States there is a time series which allows comparison not

[3] A very recent (November 1969) attempt by milk retailers in a Yorkshire town to reduce costs by rationalizing rounds has been strongly resisted by housewives; freedom to choose one's milkman is apparently a basic British right, even if it means a higher milk price, and even when all the milkmen are distributing milk from the same dairy.

only of different foods but of the changes in distributive margins over time. Table V shows the changes for the period 1958–67. The 'market basket' margin is fairly steady and there are several important foods for which the distributive margin is no greater than in 1958, in spite of increases in wages and other costs: labour costs for instance rose by 52 per cent between 1956 and 1965—but through increased productivity their share in the margin fell by 3 per cent.

On the whole the size of distributive margins does not seem to be increasing excessively, especially when we take into account the greater amount of processing and packaging that the raw material

TABLE V. *Marketing Spreads: Farmer's Share of Retail Costs for Farm-originated Food Products, 1958–67: percentage*

Year	1958	1959	1960	1961	1962	1963	1964	1965	1966	1967
Food										
Bakery and cereal products	20	19	19	20	20	20	20	21	22	21
Meat products	57	53	52	52	53	50	48	54	55	52
Fruit and vegetables fresh and processed	25	25	25	24	24	25	27	28	27	25
Dairy products	44	44	44	44	43	43	44	45	47	47
Poultry and eggs	62	57	61	58	57	57	56	57	58	53
'Market basket'	40	38	39	38	38	37	37	39	40	38

Source: USDA, *Agricultural Statistics*, 1968.

undergoes to suit the convenience of the working wife. The simplest foods which are eaten in their natural form (oranges, for example) have to be picked, taken to the packing-house, washed, inspected, graded, packed, loaded on to a lorry or rail wagon and taken to the fruit auction; thence they undergo the various distributive stages, and when finally they are sold to the consumer it would in fact have been cheaper for her to buy frozen orange juice; of 117 convenience foods investigated in the United States, 38 actually cost less than their fresh equivalents.[4]

United States evidence suggests that distributive margins have not widened unduly when costs in distribution are compared with margins or when increases in prices in other sectors of the economy are considered; for quite a large range of foodstuffs the farmers' share of retail price has not fallen in the last ten years, and in other cases

[4] United States Department of Agriculture, *Miscellaneous Publication No. 1063*, Washington, 1967.

(poultry and eggs for example) the fall in the farmers' share reflects the vastly increased productivity of food production rather than the rapacity of the distributors. British evidence is not so full; for dairy products and especially for retail milk the margin has widened, and at any rate in the latter case there is evidence of much overlapping of distributive rounds and possibility of increases in productivity if retailing were better organized and less superficially competitive.

Farmers have always felt, sometimes justly and sometimes not, that their share of consumers' expenditure is unduly low, and for this reason have combined in various ways to try to regulate marketing and to cut out some links in the distributive chain, or to obtain the profits of certain distributive sectors for themselves. The chief methods have been co-operatives and marketing boards.

Farmers' Co-operative Societies

Farmers' co-operatives date at least as far back as the twelfth century; there are records in France and Switzerland of co-operative dairies which were needed because for the making of storable cheeses milk had to be pooled from twenty very small farms. The great growth of the co-operative movement occurred, however, in the eighteenth and nineteenth centuries. The Landschaften of Silesia, co-operative sources of finance which issued bonds backed by the collective security of mortgages on the farms of their members, were some of the earliest examples, with great influence on the organization of agricultural credit in Denmark. But the pioneer of the modern European co-operative movement was a German, Friedrich Wilhelm Raiffeissen (1818–88). Raiffeissen was not a farmer, but he was concerned to improve the conditions of country people in general; his co-operatives were neighbourhood based, and based also on local knowledge of the circumstances, character and capabilities of applicants for credit. This knowledge had to be thorough as the members accepted collective unlimited liability for the debts, if any, of the co-operative.

Raiffeissen's co-operatives were multi-purpose; as well as supplying credit they were agricultural merchants, and engaged in the processing and marketing of their members' produce. The small, local, multi-purpose co-operatives have continued to be typical of Germany, and of other countries where Raiffeissen's ideas were influential; most West European countries have multi-purpose co-operatives, and also credit co-operatives and land banks in the establishment of which Raiffeissen was also an innovator.

The Danish co-operative societies may be taken as examples of successful marketing of members' produce in highly competitive conditions. The first Danish co-operatives were founded in the mid-nineteenth century, and from the beginning had a strong rural bias (as opposed to English co-operatives which drew their strength from urban workers). In the 1880s co-operative processing of milk (the centrifugal separator, invented in 1878 made this possible) was begun in the days of agricultural depression to put a reliable product on to the export market. The predominance of the export trade has made the Danish farmer willing to accept a good deal of discipline in his selling; co-operative members have to undertake to deliver all their produce to the co-operative society, and also to accept joint liability for its debts. This makes membership a much more lively affair than that of a trading co-operative whose members perhaps use only some of its facilities or make only a small part of their sales through it. When members use co-operatives as support buyers and desert them when a short-term price advantage offers elsewhere the movement is not viable; but the single farmer can do little of this kind of switch selling if his market is overseas. Now over 90 per cent of all milk products and pigs, Denmark's chief exports, are marketed through co-operatives.

Co-operatives act in other areas besides buying and selling; the supply of credit to members is important in Europe and America; technical advice and accountancy services, publicity and advertising are co-operative activities. In some cases the purchasing power of co-operatives has acted as a countervailing power against the suppliers of agricultural inputs, but in other cases co-operatives have had to enter the manufacturing market to safeguard members' supplies. So in Denmark there are co-operative owned cement works; the Netherlands has co-operatively run fertilizer plants, and in several countries co-operatives have entered the agricultural machinery field. The compounding of animal feeding-stuffs is general. This last development has recently made considerable progress in the United Kingdom where the co-operative movement in general has not been successful in marketing activities, probably because the lure of sporadic advantage in shifting market conditions elsewhere has proved too strong for the short-sighted British farmer.

Recently there have been signs that, with the help of government grants and advice, British co-operation in agriculture is beginning to develop; group production and selling are encouraged by grants, and there is assistance for co-operative use of machinery and plant. Some of the trading co-operatives which had hitherto functioned largely as general merchants, trading neither exclusively with, nor on behalf of, their members, have begun to be active in this sphere, especially in egg production, poultry and pigs. On the other side of the counter,

Agricultural Central Trading was formed by the National Farmers' Union to promote group buying of feeding-stuffs, fertilizer and other requisites for cash on favourable terms. Complete figures of the amount of trade done by groups are not available; co-operatives had in 1966 a joint turnover of well over £200 million, of which sales of feeding-stuffs and fertilizers to members, and trading in eggs and wool on behalf of members were the chief items. One recent estimate is that about £400 million a year of total trade in the items customarily handled by merchants (about 20 per cent) is now in the hands of co-operatives or groups.[5]

II. AGRICULTURAL MARKETING BOARDS

The British Experience

There would seem to be some relationship between the viable structure of farming in Britain compared with other European countries and the comparatively slow growth of the co-operative movement; British farmers have on the whole been able to afford the luxury of standing alone. There were, however, during the 1920s and early 1930s, enough symptoms of imperfection in the market for agricultural produce to make even British farmers sink their rights of individual selling; a series of reports published by the Ministry of Agriculture[6] on the marketing of agricultural produce resulted in the passing of the Agricultural Marketing Acts of 1931, extended and modified after the war by the Act of 1949. Under these Acts two-thirds of the producers of any agricultural commodity, who produce at least two-thirds of the output, may vote to set up a Marketing Board as the exclusive selling agency for that product. The proposals for establishing a Marketing Board must first be approved by the Minister of Agriculture after discussion and, if necessary, a public inquiry; they must then be ratified by Parliament. Once the Board is established its decisions become binding on all producers, whether they are in favour of it or not. This provision makes it impossible for a number of producers dominant in their local market to undermine the working of the Board's marketing arrangements, or for producers to desert the Board whenever there is the chance of a short-term gain by so doing.

The Boards established in the 1930s for milk, hops, potatoes, pigs and bacon had very different histories; the schemes for the marketing

[5] J. H. Kirk, 'Agriculture's Related Industries', in *Economic Change and Agriculture*, ed. Ashton and Rogers, Oliver & Boyd, London, 1967.

[6] Ministry of Agriculture and Fisheries, *Economic Series* 'Orange Books', 1925–48.

of pigs and bacon foundered on the unwillingness of farmers to maintain a steady flow of pigs to the bacon curers; the swings of the pig population resulted in cyclical changes in the price of pigs in the pork market, and in times of short supply the temptations of higher prices for pork proved too great for pig farmers, and these schemes broke down. The other Boards were temporarily suspended from their full functions during the war, when all marketing was via the Ministry of Food; subsequently marketing boards have been established for wool, eggs, potatoes, tomatoes and cucumbers; the Milk Marketing Boards have had their pre-war marketing powers restored, though the government has kept the power to determine both retail prices and the basic guaranteed price for a standard quantity of wholesale milk. A scheme for a marketing board for apples and pears was rejected by producers; the Minister of Agriculture has refused to ratify schemes for a marketing board for meat, and has instead set up an advisory Meat and Livestock Commission.

The differing histories of these boards reflect the different attitudes of producers of commodities; the Tomato and Cucumber Board had a short life; producers apparently considered that it served no useful purpose and preferred the chances of the open market. The housewife, confronted with the extraordinary conglomeration of sizes and shapes in these British products, and reduced often to the purchase of imported produce from retail chains to obtain a standard quality, must wonder if the demise of the Board served her best interests. Attempts similarly to dismantle the Potato Marketing Board have been defeated; the Board acts as a support buyer and controls output (in what, given the incidence of seasonal crop fluctuations, is a rather hit and miss manner) by means of acreage allotments, and has by these means stabilized producer prices. The Egg Marketing Board was from the first troubled by the identification of its brand mark with stale eggs; there was an often spurious identification of unmarked eggs with a 'country fresh' image. Producers were allowed to market a proportion of their output individually; there was little control of this, so that the Board became the residual purchaser in times of glut, when it was compelled to buy all eggs offered to it and to sell them to manufacturers. In recent years the emergence of very large egg producers who count their birds in millions and think that they can get better prices by direct sales has further undermined the Board's authority. In 1969 the Board was voted out of existence by a majority of producers, the smaller among whom are now wondering whether they will be able to face the competition of the large firms, whether they will have to sell on contract to packers or through the feeding-stuff firms which have begun to operate contracts tying sales to purchases of feeding-stuffs and if so what terms of sale they will be able to negotiate. Since the mid-1950s eggs have been very cheap—in real terms they are half their pre-war price—but this is because of the technical improvements in egg production and an element of price subsidy, not because of the marketing arrangements. It will be interesting to see if, in the next few years, egg prices and marketing arrangements bear out the views of those economists who see marketing boards as conspiracies against the consumer and predict a fall in consumer prices if marketing boards are abolished, or if production becomes concentrated in a few very large firms who are more interested in competitive advertising than in competitive price.

The Milk Marketing Boards of which there are five in the United Kingdom, have been the most successful of those so far established; to their normal marketing functions they have added the control and improvement of quality, advertising, recording of herd and individual animal performance, progeny testing, the provision of artificial insemination services using performance-tested sires, advice on herd management, accounting and economic services. It is very unlikely that these services would have been provided by competing co-operatives of producers which would inevitably have developed as local associations with less finance for research and development, and which because they would have been faced with a few oligopsonistic buyers, would have been less successful in looking after the interests of producers.

Since the war the Boards have not had restored to them the power of fixing retail prices or retail margins; they must operate within the limits of these and the wholesale price related to the government's guaranteed price. It is impossible in the circumstances to decide how the existing system of milk distribution compares in efficiency with a possible non-monopolistic system; certainly the Boards' own wholesale collection and distribution, which in 1968–9 cost less per gallon than in 1955, is a model of efficiency: in the same period competitive retail margins have more than doubled.

The Functions of Marketing Boards

There is some similarity between the functions of marketing boards and of co-operatives, so much so that it is sometimes maintained that there is nothing that a marketing board can legitimately do that a co-operative cannot also do. This is perhaps true of very large co-operatives which collect and process commodities for the export market; they are effective monopsonists as far as the producers in their area are concerned. It is not likely to be true of co-operatives selling mainly on a home market where a temporary condition of over-supply may lead to price collapse in the absence of effective support buying or methods of price maintenance. There will always be a temptation for the financially weaker co-operatives to sell, and the less competition there is from buyers the less effective will be the countervailing power of smaller producers' associations. Measures to reduce supply when there is disequilibrium in the market in the long term are notoriously difficult to bring about if there are competitive sellers; from the consumers' angle this is perhaps desirable; in theory competition in these circumstances will weed out the inefficient. In fact much will depend upon the degree of competition among buyers; there is no inevitable decrease in retail price when producers' price falls; the only result may be a widening of the retail margin. A monopolistic board whose activities are subject to government control may prove to be more effective in support buying and price stabilization for producers and at the same time less prone to indulge in brand oriented advertising than two or three large competitive firms; it is not the marketing boards who give away plastic daffodils or children's tawdry toys with their products. In the opposite conditions, when prices are high, non-monopsonistic co-operatives will have difficulty in enforcing the loyalty of members, who may be tempted to take the highest available price from other buyers.

A more serious criticism of the monopolistic marketing board is that because it has obligations to buy produce offered by all its members it may keep in being patterns of production which are inefficient; it may, for example, subsidize the production of milk in Welsh valleys remote from liquid markets by pooling transport costs for all milk purchased; this criticism of pooling arrangements has been made in recent years by an independent committee which reported in 1963 to the Milk Marketing Board,[7] and again in 1968 when some producers in the south-east of England claimed that the Board's policy of pooling transport costs discriminated against them. In both cases attempts at incorporating true transport differentials into the producer price only revealed the impossibility of logically drawing any line of demarcation short of paying each producer according to the actual day-to-day destination of his milk; obviously the imperfections of the pooling system are outweighed by the accounting complexities of a day-to-day disposal system. Pricing by 'milk-sheds', regional zones or local administrative boundaries all involve illogicalities; in areas as small as those of the British Milk Marketing Boards it may be better to operate a pool price and to

[7] Davis Committee, *Report*, Milk Marketing Board, Thames Ditton, 1963.

leave the determination of the pattern of production to the workings out of the Theorem of Comparative Advantage in factors other than that of simple location. It is of interest that the milk producers of south-east England who felt that they should receive the price benefits of proximity to a large liquid market gave as a supporting reason for their claim the higher costs of production (land prices, wage rates) which they incurred compared with producers in less populous regions. To the housewife it is a matter of indifference whether the price she pays for milk is made up of high transport cost and low other costs or low transport cost and high other costs if the final result is the same.

TABLE VI. *Realization of Various Categories of Milk, England and Wales, Year Ending March 31, 1969*

	Pence per gallon
Liquid milk	55·87
Butter	13·22
Cheese	23·05
Condensed milk	23.27
Milk powder	27·37
Cream (fresh)	27·37
(sterilized)	23·01
Other products	27·00

Source: *Dairy Facts and Figures*, Federation of United Kingdom Milk Marketing Boards, 1969.

Price discrimination by a marketing board in selling its produce could also be said to distort market conditions; the Milk Marketing Board for England and Wales, for instance, has at least eight different selling prices for milk according to its use, liquid milk fetching the highest price and butter the lowest. The Board is a monopolist in the liquid milk market, and out of its monopoly profits it finances the production of milk for manufacture; total receipts are pooled, all producers receiving the same price (except for quality premia or deductions, and a small allowance for transport). The range of prices current in the year ending March 1969 is shown in Table VI. No farmer in Britain can produce milk at the price the Board receives for milk for butter manufacture, but because of the price pooling system no producer receives the (marginal) butter price; production therefore tends to be extended beyond the optimal quantity at which marginal revenue would equal marginal cost. By differentiating its producer price month by month, the

Board tries to minimize the quantity of milk going into the less lucrative forms of production, treading delicately between the unmanageable summer glut that a flat-rate price would elicit (as has happened in the EEC) and the winter surplus that the war-time and post-war pricing policies (designed to keep up winter supplies of liquid milk in conditions of overall scarcity) were tending to produce. It seems unlikely that any organization except a discriminating monopolist and monopsonist could manage this operation with comparable efficiency.

On British evidence the Marketing Boards do not seem to have abused their monopolistic powers; they have not, for instance, been tempted to use accumulated funds for inappropriate purposes, like the Nigerian Marketing Boards of the 1950s.[8] Products marketed by the Boards have not shown undue price rises: indeed some of them—eggs, milk, potatoes—have compared well with general levels of prices, and milk producers have consistently opposed the adoption of supply management schemes which would have increased profits by raising price. Where there is genuine competitive demand, as for much fatstock, grain and horticultural products, co-operatives without mandatory powers may function just as well as marketing boards. In conditions which tend to over-supply and where buyers are few, marketing boards, accountable to the government, would seem to be the better organs of marketing.

Farmers as Buyers

Strong co-operatives, or buying groups, should be able to bargain with suppliers to the advantage of their members; they should also, by guaranteeing large sales, be welcomed by suppliers, but this has certainly not always been so. Some of the European co-operatives have been driven to enter various fields of manufacturing because of purchasing difficulties, and British buying groups, which have developed in the 1960s, have been looked upon very coldly by some of the major suppliers. In some cases farmers found that the prices that they were asked for requisites were higher through buying groups than individually. The wiser farmers stuck by their groups, and in consequence prices of many agricultural inputs have become highly competitive; in fertilizers, for example, there is no such thing as a purchase at manufacturer's list price for the farmer who shops around, and margins in this particular case have fallen so much that some merchants and trading co-operatives are actually selling at a loss. (There is naturally much hearsay in such matters, but such

8 See G. Helleiner, 'Nigerian Marketing Boards', *Economic Journal*, September 1964.

figures as are available from merchants lend credibility to this assertion. Margins which are actually less than handling costs have been recorded.) Certainly no one who has in recent years negotiated prices for feeding-stuffs, fertilizers or traded-in second-hand machinery can doubt the value of organized buying; even those farmers who do not belong to groups benefit from the competitive selling which buying groups can induce.

CHAPTER VI

International Trade in Agricultural Products

The Historical Background

An eighteenth-century statesman would have found it incredible that there should be any doubt about the propriety of government interference in the free flow of goods between countries; not only were customs duties a useful source of revenue, but regulation of trade by specific measures of quantitive control was accepted as normal. The American colonists of Great Britain did not rebel against the *principle* of taxation of goods which crossed international boundaries but at its specific application. Adam Smith (1723–90) and his successors, notably David Ricardo (1772–1823) were responsible for the formulation of the idea that the freeing of international trade from all restrictions was a means of increasing the prosperity and welfare of all trading nations. By 1810 a British statesman, William Huskisson, was writing that the commercial interest of all countries was 'most effectually consulted by leaving to every part of the world to raise those productions for which soil and climate are best adapted'. A time more suitable for the propagation of such ideas could not have been found, for Great Britain was beginning that long period of supremacy in manufacturing which lasted throughout the nineteenth century; her advantage over less industrialized countries made the maximization of the interchange of goods and services to her best interest. When to this material advantage was added the moral fervour of the anti-corn law movement the impetus to the freeing of trade from all restrictions was irresistible, and the Anglo-French Treaty of Commerce in 1860 was the first of a series of commercial treaties which by 1870 had freed international trade, especially in agricultural commodities, from all except a few minor restrictions.

At this time international trade in agricultural products was, except for tropical and semi-tropical products which were still classed as luxuries, largely carried on between the countries of

Europe. It was precisely at the time when trade barriers were dismantled that this pattern was disrupted by the advent of the iron-built steam ship, which not only shortened the time of ocean voyages and reduced their cost but also played a great part in opening up the American continent through its vast river system. Where steam ships could not go railways could; by 1880 the United States had 94,000 miles of railways, mainly across the prairies, where the new settlers were encouraged by the railway companies with undertakings to carry their crops at less than cost for a guaranteed period of years. The cost of sending a ton of grain from Chicago to London fell from £3 7s in 1873 to £1 4s in 1884. The opening up of virgin lands and the improvement of agricultural machinery (notably the self-binding reaper) provided the huge grain crops for the new modes of transport to carry to European markets. United States exports of grain increased by over 600 per cent between 1861 and 1884; grain began to come from Canada and Australia and in increased quantities from Russia. Prices fell, with small intermissions, till by the mid-1890s the price of British wheat was only 40 per cent of its level in the early 1870s.

Concurrently with the fall in grain prices livestock prices began to decline as the competition of refrigerated meat from the southern hemisphere began to be felt, but rising populations in Europe and the very availability of cheap imported feeding-stuffs meant that livestock producers did not suffer as much as did arable farmers. By the end of the nineteenth century the present pattern of international trade in temperate products was established. Britain was the great open food market of the world; North America was the chief exporter of grain, Australasia and the Argentine were the chief exporters of meat. Farmers in Britain, Denmark and Holland turned their attention to the production of livestock and dairy produce, processing the cheap grain from the newly cultivated lands, but while Holland and Denmark were dependent on agriculture for a great part of their national income, and therefore undertook a serious reorganization of methods of husbandry and marketing Britain, only 8 per cent of whose population was employed in agriculture by the turn of the century, adhered to a rigid policy of *laissez faire*. Few voices were raised against such a policy, and farmers accepted it as a fact of life, and operated with the minimum of risk, investing little in fixed capital or even in the maintenance of soil health.

The major countries of continental Europe were never ideologically committed to free trade; agriculture therefore received similar treatment to industry, and when the fall in agricultural prices began there was immediate resort to protection by tariffs or physical restrictions on trade. A level of protection of from 20 to 25 per cent was estimated as being general by 1913; when the second Great Depression of 1931 brought about catastrophic falls in agricultural prices, tariffs and other devices raised the level of protection to about 50 per cent.[1] In 1932 even Britain was at last forced by the large-scale dumping of food products (imports of these increased by 35 per cent during 1931) to abandon its free trade policy; the Imports Duties Act imposed a general tariff of 10 per cent *ad valorem* on all imports. Exceptions were made for certain raw materials and food-stuffs, the most important being wheat, maize, livestock and meat, and wool. Later in the same year the Ottawa Agreements which confirmed the exemption of Empire produce from the tariffs, gave powers to the government to impose higher duties on foreign produce which competed in British markets with Empire produce. Imports from the Empire increased at the expense of other suppliers; Denmark in particular was hit by the preference given to dairy produce from New Zealand, and to bacon products from Canada.

The Present Position

By the outbreak of the Second World War there was no country which was not in some measure regulating its external trade in agricultural commodities; the war years saw a great extension of self-sufficiency even in those countries which had previously been the largest importers—the United Kingdom, for example, raised its home production of total food requirements (measured in calories) from 30 per cent pre-war to 40 per cent in 1944. When the war and the immediate post-war years of food scarcity were over, international trade in temperate agricultural commodities resumed much of its traditional pattern. The major changes are the vast overall increase in output, and the strengthening of the position of the United States and Canada as dominant suppliers in the world grain trade, while Australia's share has declined from one-third in the immediate pre-war period to one-eighth, and Russia is only intermittently a seller on world markets, and in some years has been a major importer. Japan has now overtaken the United Kingdom as the chief importer of wheat and flour, and of coarse grains for animal feeding-stuffs (Table I), and is beginning to take more meat and dairy products from Australia and New Zealand. In Europe the establishment of the European Economic Community has created a largely self-sufficient entity for temperate agricultural products whose policy of price support for its own farmers and export subsidization has created difficulties for traditional exporters (such as Denmark) and

[1] H. Liepmann, *Tariff Levels*, George Allen & Unwin, London, 1938.

TABLE IA. *Changes in the Value of Agricultural Trade 1961 to 1966 (in US dollars)*

(a) *Exports*   (Selected countries)

Country	Chief exports	$000,000 value of total agricultural exports	
		1961	1966
Denmark	Meat and meat products Dairy products	9,621	12,870
France	Cereals: Wine.	12,757	20,252
Italy	Fruits and vegetables	8,038	19,667
Netherlands	Meat, dairy products, vegetables	14,224	19,263
United Kingdom	Agricultural requisites and prepared foods	8,335	11,285
USSR	Textile fibres, wood products	13,907	13,864
Canada	Cereals	13,217	20,500
USA	Cereals: tobacco	51,713	71,250
Argentina	Cereals: meat	11,560	14,741
Brazil	Coffee	10,302	13,973
India	Tea	6,743	6,269

Source: FAO *Trade Yearbook*, Vol. 21, 1967.

TABLE IB

(b) *Imports*

Country	Chief imports	$000,000 value of total agricultural imports	
		1961	1966
Belgium/Luxembourg	Cereals: textile fibres	9,650	13,329
France	Fruits and vegetables: textile fibres	24,361	29,915
West Germany	Fruits and vegetables: cereals	41,861	52,124
Italy	Cereals	16,468	27,499
Netherlands	Cereals	10,268	14,444
United Kingdom	Meat: fruits and vegetables: cereals	57,014	60,094
USSR	Cereals	12,817	21,561
Canada	Fruits and vegetables	8,534	10,098
USA	Coffee	47,311	56,687
India	Cereals	5,984	10,691
Japan	Cereals, sugar	19,111	33,546

Source: ibid.

as surpluses of some commodities pile up is beginning to threaten the markets of exporters of other agricultural products; for instance, New Zealand was alarmed in 1969 by the sudden rise in imports to the British market of cheese from France and Holland, and Canada and the United States which are low-cost producers of wheat can hardly view with pleasure the appearance in British ports of European wheat the price of which on the home market is £40 per ton (98·75 dollars per metric ton) but which is sold at less than the British minimum import price of £22 19s per ton.[2] The EEC countries are not by any means the only exporters of subsidized commodities; Australian butter, Canadian cheese, Danish dairy produce and bacon—the list of temperate foodstuffs entering world trade with some sort of subsidy either direct, or in the form of producer subsidies or differentiation between export and domestic prices is long. Some producers are, of course, more efficient than others; and some products—Canadian grain, New Zealand butter—are sold on world markets at genuine cost of production. But in the face of universal government management of markets and price supports it is impossible to say what the true, competitive, world market price for any commodity would be; to assume that the present price of the lowest-cost world suppliers would be the world price if all restrictions on trade were abolished, is to assume that in some countries agriculture is being carried on in conditions of constant costs, so that marginal cost would equal average cost, and production could be expanded indefinitely to fill the gap left by the elimination of high-cost producers without any increase in the present lowest supply price. This is manifestly improbable; New Zealand, for example, now supplies about 37 per cent of the British market for butter. This represents 85 per cent of all New Zealand's butter exports; seriously to inconvenience all the possible alternative suppliers of butter on international markets New Zealand would have at least to double her production at constant prices, which her already intensive farms could not do. In the absence of trade barriers the world price for agricultural commodities would therefore settle down somewhere between the supply prices of present high-cost and low-cost producers. Where this would be is anyone's guess; it is certainly not the French price, as was suggested in the once much-discussed Baumgartner–Pisani plan for regulation of international trade in agricultural commodities.

The Consequences of Trade Restrictions

The effect of the imposition of a tariff or levy is in general to

[2] *Farmers' Weekly*, March 14, 1969.

I

reduce the volume of trade between two countries by raising the price of imports. A tariff *ad valorem* will increase the price of the imported good by a greater amount as the world price rises (Fig. 1a). If the world market price falls, either because there is over-supply or because of price supports in exporting countries, the *ad valorem*

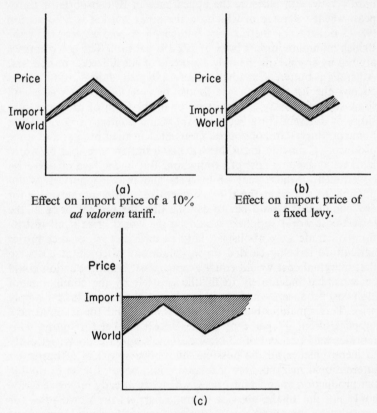

(a)
Effect on import price of a 10% *ad valorem* tariff.

(b)
Effect on import price of a fixed levy.

(c)

Effect on import price of a variable levy.

Fig. 1.

The effects of tariffs and fixed and variable levies on import prices.

tariff will be of less protection to home producers than will be a levy, either fixed (Fig. 1b) or variable (Fig. 1c). The latter is chosen when the aim is to achieve a fixed domestic price for a commodity which is both home-produced and imported. One curious measure of import control is the minimum import price first introduced by the British Government in 1964; this was designed to reduce the cost of deficiency payments to British cereal growers by raising the import price of grains above the world price by asking exporting countries not to sell grain in Britain at less than a certain agreed price. This measure had the welfare dis-benefits of a variable levy without the usual offsetting benefit to the importing government's revenues.

Export subsidies have the contrary effect to tariffs and levies of reducing the price of commodities on world markets (Fig. 2). The extent of the change in the volume of trade which import levies or tariffs and export subsidies bring about depends on the relative elasticities of demand for and supply of the commodity, both in the

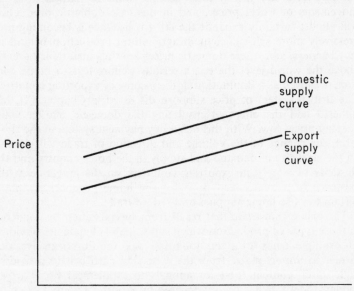

Fig. 2.
The effect of an export subsidy on World Supply Price.

importing and exporting countries and in other countries which compete in world markets. Demand for a commodity from any one exporter will be inelastic when there are few or no alternative sources of supply; this case will be met rarely except in the very short term, or when international trade is disrupted by war. More usually, total demand in any one importing country for a commodity will be inelastic but the demand schedule facing a single exporter will be elastic, in the absence of quota arrangements. The imposition of a levy on imports when total demand is inelastic will raise prices, yield revenue to the importing government, but have little effect on the volume of trade. The direction of trade between the importer and suppliers will be altered if some of them assist exports by subsidies and others do not; the international market for butter (which is in effect the United Kingdom market) has shown such trade diversion at various times since the Second World War, when subsidized exports from countries with temporary surpluses diverted trade from New Zealand.

In the longer term the trade-restricting or trade-diverting effects of import levies will be considerable, as higher prices in importing countries encourage home production; it is possible by the use of variable levies completely to isolate the domestic market from the movements of world prices, and in this case domestic production will almost certainly expand; the EEC for instance is becoming progressively more self-sufficient in agricultural production behind its levy barriers, and where domestic prices are thus maintained greatly above the world level there is a serious welfare loss to home consumers as well as a diminution in the income of exporting countries. The British system of price support, discussed in Chapter VII, has hitherto had the effect of insulating the domestic market while keeping prices low. With this deficiency payment system in the short term, the change in the volume and direction of trade will depend on the elasticity of demand and supply in the home country and the elasticity of supply in exporting countries; in the longer term the existence of a guaranteed price for the home producer is almost certain to raise home supplies and reduce trade.

The gains from trade that result from specialization by countries in those types of production which suit soil and climate are obvious; for example it has for a very long time paid the European livestock farmer to import maize from the American corn belt to provide a high starch content food for animals to supplement home-grown fodder; the maize has been purchased by exports of animal products or industrial products (or first one and then the other, as when Danish farmers export their pork products to Britain which in turn exports industrial goods to America). From the Theorem of Comparative Advantage we learn that even if one of two countries is superior to the other in both agricultural and industrial production, it will still be to the advantage of both to specialize in that sector in which their comparative advantage is greatest (and disadvantage less), and to exchange goods by mutual trade. The almost universal policy of protection for both industry and agriculture distorts the pattern of production which would emerge if natural and comparative advantage were allowed to operate freely, and for agricultural products protection is more often in the form of variable levies, import quotas or support of the domestic produce rather than *ad valorem* tariffs so that it is difficult to estimate its extent. It has been suggested that British agriculture enjoys a rate of protection of about 15 per cent, comparable with that of industry,[3] and that in the EEC agricultural policies give protection equivalent to a 30 per cent tariff.[4]

In these circumstances the position of the traditional exporters is difficult. The reaction of New Zealand has been to look for markets in Japan and other developing countries; Denmark has supported its agriculture,[5] reduced its imports of grain, rationalized farm structure and diversified its economy (agricultural products now account for only 36 per cent of Denmark's foreign earnings compared with over 60 per cent in the 1950s). The United States has taken steps to restrict production, and has exported vast quantities of agricultural produce on concessional terms to developing countries.

The position of importing countries has been anomalous in that while it has been possible for them to import freely the subsidized products of other countries, yet they have continued to give support to home agriculture. During the 1950s there was much discussion in Britain about the desirability or otherwise of the level of support then obtaining; many economists considered that Britain should revert to her traditional role of being largely dependent on overseas supplies of food, since resources could be more profitably employed in industrial production than in the expansion of home agriculture. Only Professor E. A. G. Robinson consistently argued that balance of payments problems would make the expansion of home agricultural production necessary.[6] The experience of the 1960s has not only borne out Professor Robinson's predictions but has emphasized the inherent dangers of placing too much reliance on the continued competitiveness of exporting industry as the source of payment for essential food-stuffs. It seems most unlikely that the traditional free-trade policy will be accepted in the future: the elasticity of demand for industrial products is likely to diminish as the primary exporters diversify their economies.

Measures to Stabilize International Trade

Britain has accepted some obligations towards its long-standing

[3] J. Hutchinson, *Presidential Address* to the Agricultural Section of the British Association, 1969.

[4] G. U. Papi and C. C. Nunn, eds., *Economic Problems of Agriculture in Industrial Societies*, Macmillan, 1969, p. 45.

[5] Agricultural support amounted by 1969 to 2 per cent of Denmark's GNP, compared with Great Britain's 0·8 per cent.

[6] *Agriculture in the British Economy*, ICI, 1957; 'The Cost of Agricultural Import Saving', *Three Banks Review*, December 1958.

suppliers of agricultural products who in fact suffer more than the British farmer from the erratic and unpredictable dumping of commodities. After the second catastrophic fall in the price of butter on the London market in three years an agreement was concluded in 1961 between the United Kingdom Government and the governments of her traditional suppliers for the import of butter to be controlled by annually renewable quotas; a similar market-sharing agreement for bacon was concluded in 1964 and renewed in 1969. Sugar imports have been controlled since 1951 by the Commonwealth Sugar Agreement which provides for guaranteed imports from Commonwealth sugar-producing countries at prices 'which shall be reasonably remunerative to efficient producers'; Canada participates in this agreement as an importer.

The value of these agreements is in their elimination of the erratic dumping of produce which is in temporary surplus elsewhere; the butter quotas have, however, had the effect of shifting the incidence of subsidized imports to other dairy produce, first cheese, until this became the subject of an anti-dumping application which led to the voluntary acceptance of quotas by exporting countries in 1969, and then dried milk, about which the British Milk Marketing Boards are currently (autumn 1969) complaining. In spite of such difficulties, market-sharing agreements such as these have had stabilizing effects in international markets: the price of butter on the London market in fact now shows almost complete stability.

International agreements covering all marketings of agricultural commodities have not been easy to negotiate or particularly successful. The outstanding success has been the International Grains Agreement first negotiated in 1953 and renewable periodically; this, in effect sets minimum and maximum prices for world trade in wheat, in relation to the price of United States No. 2 hard red winter wheat at Gulf of Mexico ports. This agreement has been successful because the United States and Canada have been willing to stockpile wheat in times of surplus production and to release stocks on commercial and concessional terms in times of shortage. Other international agreements have been of very limited application; that for sultanas has set minimum prices; that for olive oil has attempted to control quality. The International Coffee Agreement broke down because some participating countries continued to sell above their quotas; Brazil, the main producer, discontinued its planned destruction of coffee trees because other countries continued to plant coffee. There is, however, a new agreement now operating fixing export quotas on the basis of production in the period 1959–66; increase in quotas will be tied to adherence to production 'ceilings'; the problem of over-production of coffee is to be tackled by the use of funds to promote export diversification.

The paucity of international agreements for the regulation of trade in agricultural commodities follows from the difficulties of enforcing and financing such agreements. Enforcement of quotas on sales is almost impossible when it is to the interest of each country to sell as much as it can; financing of buffer stocks is equally impossible when the chief exporters are primarily agricultural countries, since their sources of finance will be the more limited at those times when it is necessary, because of falling prices, to stockpile the potential exports. It is only when the chief exporters are wealthy industrial countries, such as the United States and Canada in the case of cereals, that stockpiling becomes feasible.

Developing Countries and International Trade

The developing countries are mainly exporters of tropical agricultural products. In general their exports have not suffered from the discriminatory practices that have distorted international trade in temperate products; some countries do impose revenue duties on tropical products such as tea and coffee, which tend to reduce trade or to discriminate between exporting countries, but in general, tropical products do not compete with those of the advanced countries and so do not attract the levies, quotas and other trade restrictions that affect temperate products. They do, however, in some cases compete with temperate products which are themselves the object of price support; so United States support for rice production may injure tropical rice exporters; sugar is a supported crop in almost all temperate countries; price supports in Europe and the United States for oilseeds may inhibit the increased production of vegetable oils in the traditional tropical exporting countries in the future (this has not happened hitherto since the market for all types of vegetable oil has been expanding).

The chief exports of some of the developing countries are non-food agricultural products such as cotton and rubber; competition for these products comes not from other agricultural products but from synthetic substitutes. Present low prices for these and other tropical products are in many cases (cocoa, coffee, rubber) the result of heavy plantings in the early and mid-1950s when prices were high; the long production period and the long life of the mature plantations means that though production has outstripped demand it is difficult to reduce output.

The problems of the developing countries as importers are those of insufficient foreign exchange and a variable and sometimes desperate need for food imports. The former can be dealt with only in the context of general policies of aid and of admission of industrial goods from developing countries to the markets of the developed world; the latter have been met mainly by the United States, which in the 1960s has been shipping about one-quarter of its total agricultural exports on concessionary terms under the Agricultural Trade Development and Assistance Act of 1954 (usually known as Public Law 480). Some economists have maintained that such food aid inhibits the development of the native agriculture of the developing countries; it seems, however, from the experience of the last two years, in which, helped by good weather, food output has very rapidly increased in countries which were among the most seriously deficient, that the availability of food aid has not been an inhibiting factor. India and Pakistan who have been the chief recipients of food aid have increased food output to the point at which they expect to be self-supporting in food grains by 1970.

Whether this target will be reached and for how long it will be maintained depends on the growth of populations. One estimate[7] is that grain production in the less developed countries must almost treble its 1961 level by the year 2000 and that this will not be possible, so that a gap of about 70 million tons per annum will remain to be filled by imports. OECD projections which extend to 1985 foresee a surplus of 120 million tons in the developed countries by that year; so the world's food-producing resources can meet the foreseeable need, but the distribution of food depends on international goodwill and common sense in spheres beyond that of agricultural economics.

[7] Lester R. Brown, *Man, Land and Food*, USDA, 1965.

CHAPTER VII

States and Farmers

All governments have explicit policies towards agriculture; this is perhaps worthy of remark since there are in most countries large sectors of the economy towards which governments do not have explicit policies; in particular the service trades, with which agriculture has more in common than with manufacturing industry in organization and structure are often left to sort out their problems by the working of market forces. Farmers are not so treated for a variety of reasons.

First, no government can afford to allow its country's agriculture to decline to that point at which food supplies might be in jeopardy in time of war, disruption of international transport or severe balance of payments problems. This may be called the 'strategic' reason for controlling or supporting the level of agricultural production. Some countries aim at a specified proportion of food production from home agriculture; Austria, Norway, Sweden, Switzerland, all of which would be vulnerable in time of war among their neighbours, aim at a certain degree of strategic self-sufficiency; this is less than total self-sufficiency—in Sweden, for example, the current proportion aimed at is 80 per cent—but it is enough to provide an insurance against international cataclysm. The United Kingdom Government, in framing agricultural policy in the 1947 Agriculture Act, stated that the aim of legislation was to secure the production in the home country of 'such part of the nation's food and other agricultural produce as in the national interest it is desirable to produce'. This sensibly vague phrase left to succeeding governments a latitude in agricultural policy which they have successfully exploited.

Secondly, government policy may be directed towards the farming industry itself, either to maintain or increase farmers' incomes, to maintain the numbers of those employed in agriculture, or conversely to decrease them. Such policies are found both in countries where agriculture supplies only part of home demand for food, and in exporting countries. In this aspect of policy also the British Government in 1947 committed itself to no more than a vague aspiration to secure 'adequate remuneration' to those engaged in agriculture—and government itself was to decide what constitutes such adequate return.

Within these two broad categories—the attempt to achieve a certain level or proportion of agricultural production, and the attempt to maintain a certain standard of living for all, or some proportion of the present agricultural population—we may distinguish two types of policy.

Policies of Scarcity

Wherever agricultural production is insufficient to meet demand, certain kinds of policy designed to induce increases in output are found. At the present time the countries applying such policies are mainly those of the less developed regions.

Some of the factors which militate against increased production in such countries were noted in Chapter I. They are briefly:

1. Deficiencies in the infrastructure and in social provision; examples are lack of organized marketing, so that farmers are at the mercy of local merchants, who are often local monopsonists who can conceal from the farmers the true state of demand for their products; poor transport, so that the market is spatially limited; lack of education, so that the dissemination of knowledge of improved methods is difficult.

2. Deficiencies in agricultural structure; where there is much share cropping, or where production is divided between large extensively farmed latifundia and tiny subsistence plots (as in Latin America) or where holdings in general are too small to produce much more than the bare requirements of the farmer and his family, it may not be possible to achieve improvements in output without measures of land reform.

3. Lack of money for more or better farm requisites such as fertilizer, improved strains of seed and so on. This is especially limiting since in the developing countries farming requisites are costly; fertilizer, for example, is usually three or four times as dear in real terms as in the developed countries.

4. Dear credit for purchases of requisites; in many cases the merchants who buy the harvested crops are also the lenders of money, and it is not unknown for interest rates of 5 or 6 per cent per *month* to be demanded. The crop is pledged to the merchant before it is harvested, and there is no escape from the monetary bondage.

5. Severe instability of prices; most farmers must sell their crops as soon as they are harvested, since they have neither the knowledge nor the resources to hang on to some of their produce till prices rise.

Typically prices are at their lowest immediately after harvest, sometimes as much as five or six times lower than in the preceding weeks.
If the harvest is good the price fall will be catastrophic; if the harvest
is poor the small farmers will have little or nothing to sell.

Clearly the policies which would ameliorate these conditions
depend on the competence of governments and on the availability
of finance. General policies of development would include improvements of the infrastructure and of education. The magnitude of the
latter task in some of the less developed countries is well illustrated
by the series of articles currently appearing in the *Solomon Islands
Farmer*, a government publication of the utmost simplicity, which
aims at telling the farmers (presumably through their literate
children) that if you do not give pigs enough food they will not
grow, and that if you tether them to a tree and never move the
tether they will eventually die.

In such circumstances governments sometimes resort to compulsion to enforce measures of good husbandry. One example of this is
the Gezira Scheme in the Sudan, where between the White and Blue
Niles an area of 2 million hectares is being brought into production,
mostly through irrigation works; tenants of the Gezira lands have
yearly tenancies dependent upon their following an approved scheme
of cultivation and cropping. The United Arab Republic similarly
controls the areas of land which may be put into cotton, and insists
on a minimum acreage of wheat (of which it is a large importer). It
is not always easy to compel farmers to abandon inadequate or out-
dated methods, or to compel them to market their produce; some
of the countries of Eastern Europe have had to modify or abandon
plans for, for example, the establishment of collective farms in the
face of the opposition, evasions and foot-dragging of the agricultural
population. In the USSR, neither compulsion nor exhortation has
been enough to induce a sufficient expansion of agricultural production, and the prices of livestock and dairy products have had to be
raised in an attempt to increase output.

Compulsion of another kind may be exerted by governments who
impose such heavy taxes on agriculture that farmers have to increase
output simply to pay their taxes; the classic case of this is that of
Japan in the late nineteenth century, where it has been estimated that
the annual rate of growth of agricultural production between 1878
and 1917 was 2·3 per cent, and the total increase in net agricultural
output per unit of cultivated area was 80 per cent. During this
period the land tax yielded much the greater part of Japan's total
tax revenue (over 80 per cent of tax revenue from 1888 till the end

of the century, this being over 20 per cent of agriculture's total income). It is very doubtful whether such methods would be universally successful; in the Argentine, for example, in the 1950s, export taxes on meat which were designed to effect transfer payments from the agricultural to the industrial sectors merely had the effect of reducing exports; the Argentinians ate the meat and avoided the taxes.

During the Second World War the British Government took powers to compel farmers to plough up grassland, and to plant specified acreages of potatoes; farmers were placed in three classes according to their standards of husbandry; those in the 'C' class were placed under supervision by the County War Agricultural Executive Committees. Under siege conditions these measures of compulsion were accepted, but the continuance of the supervisory powers and of the legislative power of dispossession into peace time was bitterly resented. Such measures were probably inescapable as long as profit margins in farming were large enough to allow the inefficient to get by and as long as maximum production was essential. They became otiose once food was freely available, but it was not until 1958 that the last compulsory sanction—that of dispossession of tenants whose landlords could obtain certificates from the Agricultural Executive Committees that they were farming badly—was ended. Their place was taken by measures of price control and guarantee and by production incentives, to the consideration of which we must now turn.

Production Incentives

The most important and widely used incentive to production is the guaranteed price (see Chapter IV). Because of the 'stickiness' of factors of production, alterations in price alone may not be enough to change the pattern or the amount of production; even where increases in price do induce increases in output this may not in itself help the farmers if there is no concomitant policy of price stabilization, since changes in supply may be irreversible in the short or medium term, and without a policy of storage or planned marketings instability of agricultural incomes may merely be aggravated by price-induced increases in output. Policies of price guarantee must not be undertaken, therefore, without regard to the orderly marketing of produce, or to the price elasticity of demand for produce; price alone, as we saw in Chapter IV, is not always a sufficient means for the attainment of regular equilibrium between demand and supply.

Governments therefore usually supplement price policies with other production incentives.

A common incentive is the provision of *cheap credit*; this makes the adoption of new techniques easier, but it sometimes has the effect of raising the price of agricultural inputs; this applies especially to land, so that the position of established farmers may be improved at the expense of newcomers to agriculture. 'Cheap' is, of course, a relative term, and in the less developed countries the provision of credit at cheaper rates than those prevailing can only enhance the possibilities of improving productive methods.

In some cases agriculture receives *preferential treatment in taxation*; for example, the United Kingdom exempts farm land and buildings from local rates, and applies reduced rates of estate duty to agricultural land. (This is to some extent simply a recognition of the fact that agricultural land is raw material as well as private transferable capital; other industries where the typical unit of organization is the public company are not, of course, liable to estate duty.)

In some developing countries the *provision of consumer goods* as an inducement to increased marketings of agricultural products is advocated; the countries of the West have no similar need; though their industrial revolutions were preceded by revolutions in agriculture there was already a sufficient supply of craftsman-made goods to arouse the cupidity of earlier generations of farmers and their wives, and this is probably true of all but societies so primitive that they have no division of labour.

The most common form of production incentive is the *subsidizing of the purchase of selected inputs*, and the provision of *grants for improvements* to land and to fixed equipment. Into the latter category come grants to provide or improve irrigation works, for land drainage, for farm buildings, machinery, the supply of electricity and telephones, the improvements of farm roads and so on.

In the United Kingdom such production grants have increased in importance compared with guarantees since the Agricultural Act of 1957 (Table I). The scope of those currently operative is shown in Table II.

TABLE I. *Proportions of Exchequer Support for Agriculture by Types of Grant and Guarantee*

	1955–6	1961–2	1968–9
		£ million	
Price guarantees	14·3	225·5	137·3
Production grants	58·0	108·1	130·2

Source: Annual Review and Determination of Guarantees, HMSO, annually.

The aim of production grants and subsidies is primarily to increase total or selected items of production; the secondary aim is to educate farmers in the use of improved methods of husbandry. In judging

TABLE II. *United Kingdom Production Grants and Subsidies to Agriculture 1968–9*

	£ million
(1) Fertilizers	35·0
Lime	5·2
Ploughing	0·5
Field beans	1·6
Field drainage (other than tiling)	0·6
Calves	27·3
Beef cows	4·5
Hill cows	10·7
Hill sheep	6·7
Winter keep	4·6
Small farmers	1·9
Farm business records	1·5
Crofting (cropping)	1·5
Other	1·2
Total I	101·8
(2) Field drainage (tiling)	4·9
Water supply	0·5
Livestock rearing land	0·8
Hill land	1·8
Farm improvements	14·8
Farm structure	2·2
Investment inventives	10·3
Crofting improvements	0·3
Other	0·2
Total II	35·8

(1) Taken into account. (2) Excluded in calculating the annual value of guarantees.

Source: *Annual Review and Determination of guarantees 1969*, HMSO

their effectiveness it is too facile to refer to the practice of the most efficient farmers; the United Kingdom ploughing grant has been criticized, for instance, because permanent grass has been shown to be in some circumstances as productive as temporary grass (grass grown after ploughing, from specially selected seed). It is true that with optimum management this is so, but the tradition of management of permanent grass was, before the war and, indeed, all too often still, deplorable, with no use of fertilizer, or only lime and slag at infrequent intervals. Crops, however, were treated with more respect, and to treat grass as a crop by ploughing and re-seeding was the only way to improve its management. This grant is now being phased out; in the present state of agricultural knowledge it is possibly no longer necessary. It is similarly clear that some other production grants could now be abandoned; efficient farmers would apply fertilizers in the absence of grant, and would grow break crops where needed in the absence of field beans grant. But these aids to farming would become marginally less attractive if prices remained at present levels, and taking farmers as a whole it is certain that in such circumstances output would fall if production grants were eliminated. In the last ten years margins in British farming have appreciably tightened, and one of the first casualties of the more stringent economic climate has been the use of lime, which has fallen to 60 per cent of its level of ten years ago. Lime is a persistent fertilizer, a deficiency in which shows only gradually; in this case it is arguable that an increased lime subsidy would have avoided this deterioration in farming practice. The alternative of an all-round increase in the prices of agricultural commodities is an exceedingly blunt instrument, helping efficient and inefficient alike. Production grants, though primarily instruments for raising output, still have uses in advanced agricultures as alternatives to higher prices.

Policies of Surplus

Most developed countries have adopted special policies toward agriculture in times of agricultural surplus; the aim of these policies has been to shield domestic agriculture from the effects of world price falls, and the preferred method has usually been the regulation of imports by quotas or tariffs. This type of protectionist policy aims at the divorce of domestic and world price levels; it is traditional in Europe, and is the accepted policy of the European Economic Community. The United Kingdom, the United States, and countries dependent on agricultural exports, have adopted other policies.

The EEC Common Agricultural Policy

The basis of the common agricultural policy (CAP) which was adopted by the EEC in 1962 is that a free-trade area in agricultural produce was to be established among the member countries: this was necessary to level food prices (and therefore industrial costs) throughout the community. This was not to be done all at once, but at intervals by groups of commodities. The first agreement, on cereals, was reached only after long and hard bargaining in 1964, and became operative in 1967; the difficulty was to reconcile the interests of the major and comparatively low-cost producer, France, with those of the high-cost producer and major importer, Germany. In the end the agreed price was set, with variations representing transport costs to the area of major deficiency, at a level high enough to keep the high-cost producers in business; this meant that prices for livestock products, for which cereals are inputs, were also set at

TABLE III. *Degree of Self-sufficiency in Food Products in the European Economic Community (percentage)*

	1958–9	1970 (estimated)
Wheat	91	107
Coarse grains	78	78
Beef and veal	92	94
Pork	101	100
Dairy produce		
(butter)	99	103
(cheese)	99	100
Eggs	90	100
Potatoes	100	100
Sugar	108	104
Vegetables	105	104
Fruit	88	89
Fats and oils	41	50

Source: C. Moutou, 'The EEC and the Move to self-sufficiency in Food Production', in *Economic Problems of Agriculture in Industrial Societies*, ed. G. U. Papi and C. C. Nunn, 1969.

high levels. The result has been a considerable increase in production, which has completely undermined any chance of the CAP's functioning as was originally intended.

This original plan was for the protection of the home market by means of variable levies on imports from outside the Community. From the proceeds of these levies price support payments were to be made to producers, the rest of the cost of maintaining the agreed price level being borne by the market. The price at which imports were to be allowed into the Community (the 'threshold' price) was to be linked to a desired or 'target' price. If production increased to such an extent that prices fell below the target, then support buying was to begin at an 'intervention' price, that is a wholesale price set at a pre-determined level below the target price. Some of the income from levies was also to be used for measures of marketing improvements, and farm reorganization in problem areas (Guidance Policies).

This plan would have been workable in a Community in which the general level of imports was high enough to yield a sufficient income from levies to provide funds for support buying; but the EEC was already, at its inception, very largely self-sufficient in agricultural produce (Table III). The increasing production encouraged by high prices has meant that the Community now has surpluses of dairy produce, wheat, sugar and vegetables. Only meat and feed grains (maize) among temperate products are imported in sufficient quantities to yield an appreciable levy income; the funds which are handled by the European Agricultural Guidance and Guarantee Fund (known from its French initials as FEOGA) have had to be supplemented by direct payments from member governments, and have been mainly used for price support, not for improvements of structure.

Between its establishment in 1961 and November 1968, FEOGA handled funds amounting to 2,032 million units of account (the common unit of account is the equivalent of one dollar's worth of gold). This was collected and disbursed in accordance with the proportions of agricultural produce imported and exported by each country, and France, as the largest exporter, benefited most, while Germany which, like Britain, imports much of its food, supplied the major share of the payments (Table IV). The budget for the year ending December 1969 is expected to exceed the total for the previous seven years together (2,437 million units of account) for as production increases without a corresponding increase in consumption, the cost of maintaining agricultural prices mounts. The chance of increasing home consumption of food is negligible; as was seen in Chapter III the income and price elasticities of demand for food are low in the short term, so that significant increases in consumption could be obtained only by very large price cuts; but consumer price cuts are ruled out by the very nature of the policy of price support, since in the absence of sufficient income from levies cuts in market prices could be made only if farm prices were also cut, or if direct government support were increased.

These seemingly insoluble difficulties have called in question the efficiency of the EEC system of agricultural support. At this point it may be well to examine the British system, which relies on direct government expenditure, and then to discuss its differences from the

K

TABLE IV. *EEC Members' Contributions and Repayments to the European Agricultural Fund, to December 31, 1968*

(Million dollars)

	Contributions			Repayments		
	(a) Guarantee	(b) Guidance	(a+b) per cent	(a) Guarantee	(b) Guidance	(a+b) per cent
Belgium	156	23	8·7	95	15	4·9
France	436	82	25·8	875	44	41·1
West Germany	436	82	30·5	875	44	16·1
Italy	413	64	23·9	306	150	23·3
Luxembourg	5	1	0·2	1	3	0·3
Netherlands	200	27	10·9	303	16	14·3
	1,748	284	100	1,784	284	100·0

Source: European Community, November 1968.

EEC system and how far either system might be applicable to different countries.

The Agricultural Policy of the United Kingdom

We saw in Chapters V and VI that even before the war the United Kingdom's traditional policy of free trade in agricultural products had been modified in the years of depression by the imposition of some tariffs, by the regulation of marketing and by some measures of price support, notably for wheat. During the war years and until 1947 a system of guaranteed prices for all produce was operated, and in that year the Agriculture Act, though vague and ambiguous in phrasing, clearly committed the Government to continued support of agriculture; the level of price support was to be reviewed annually by the Government in consultation with farmers' representatives— this policy had already been adopted in 1944—and the Government undertook to buy the whole output of certain products at guaranteed prices. Because of continuing world shortages of food, a target of expansion of agricultural production to 50 per cent higher than the pre-war level was set, to be reached in 1951–2, and this was in fact achieved.

By the mid-1950s, world food supplies had become much more plentiful; the then Government had gradually dismantled the controls over marketing which had operated during the years of shortage, and from 1954 it re-adopted the pre-war method of price support by means of deficiency payments. This method allows market price to be determined by the interplay of demand and supply; if the price falls below the level which government considers necessary to maintain home output and the incomes of British farmers, then the difference between the free market price and the desired price is made up to farmers by direct exchequer payment. These deficiency payments are the distinguishing feature of the British system of agricultural support.

The method of administering deficiency payments varies from one product to another; for grains it is paid on the acreage grown, and is determined by the difference between the guaranteed price and the average market price. This means that the individual farmer benefits if he can secure better than average market prices for his crop, either by quality differentials (hence the continued value of a good malting sample) or by delaying marketing till the post-harvest period of low prices is past. Some of the intricacies of deficiency payments for fatstock were noted in Chapter IV; the involved arrangements for abatements and supplements for fatstock and of the 'middle band'

K*

for pigs are meant to induce orderly marketing and to discourage too high levels of output.

Under the provisions of the 1947 Agriculture Act, home production of food had expanded till by 1957 it was 60 per cent above its pre-war level. In that year the Government introduced a new Agriculture Act which, among other provisions, tied future governments to the maintenance of agricultural support in total to a level which might not fall in any one year by more than 2½ per cent, and for any single product by not more than 4 per cent. Emphasis moved from a policy of expanding total output to one of 'selective expansion'. Successive governments have used their powers to alter prices to shift the balance of production between commodities as some foods have become plentiful on international markets while others, notably beef, have remained in short supply.

As food surpluses grew in the developed world the deficiency payments system came under pressure; with few restrictions on imports into the United Kingdom overseas producers were able to market their surpluses in Britain, often at dumped prices; legislation to prevent dumping was cumbersome and slow, so that in the later 1950s and the early 1960s prices of basic foodstuffs on the British market fell; correspondingly the cost of deficiency payments rose (Table V). The British Government tackled this problem by two methods; first, it extended to other commodities the system of 'standard quantities' which already applied to milk, that is, it no longer guaranteed a price for all home output of a commodity but only for a certain desired quantity; pigs and eggs were subject to regulations linking price with desired level of output, and in 1964 the standard quantity concept was applied to cereals. Secondly, governments have sought to regulate the level of imports, by market-sharing agreements for butter, bacon and cheese, by import controls for potatoes and by the imposition of variable levies designed to maintain a minimum import price for cereals.

It will be clear that the fact that British agriculture was supplying only part of the nation's requirements in most food products made the Government's application of such policies easier, in that the desired reductions in total supply could be shared among British farmers and all regular suppliers of imported food, so that the market was not severely restricted for any one set of suppliers. For foods where home supplies were almost 100 per cent of needs (eggs are the most important case), unit guarantees were cut without the possibility of a compensating increase in market shares; increasing economies of scale in the poultry industry have meant that with falling unit returns many smaller producers have had to leave the industry.

TABLE V. *Deficiency Payments to United Kingdom Producers: Relationship Between Unit Subsidy and Total Returns*

	1960–1		1962–3		1965–6		1967–8	
Fat cattle (per live cwt)	s	d	s	d	s	d	s	d
(a) Market value	142	9	137	4	175	7¾	162	1¼
(b) Unit subsidy	13	11	28	0¾	3	10¼	26	10¾
(c) Total return	156	8	169	0¾	184	0	189	0
(b) as percentage of (c)*	10·0		20·0		2·0		13·0	
Fat sheep (per lb. st. d.c.w.)								
(a) Market value	2	6¾	2	4¾	3	0	2	10
(b) Unit subsidy		7¾		9		2½		5¾
(c) Total return	3	2½	3	1¾	3	2½	3	3¾
(b) as percentage of (c)	19·0		24·0		6·0		15·0	
Fat pigs (per score d.w.)								
(a) Market value	39	4¾	32	10½	35	8¼	44	9¾
(b) Unit subsidy	6	3¼	12	11½	8	4¼	3	0¾
(c) Total return	45	8	45	10	44	0½	47	10½
(b) as percentage of (c)	13·7		28·0		19·0		6·0	
Wheat (per cwt)								
(a) Market value	18	10½	17	11	21	0	21	6½
(b) Unit subsidy	8	0½	9	5¼	3	7¾	4	4
(c) Total return	26	11	27	4	24	7¾	25	10½
(b) as percentage of (c)	30·0		35·0		14·0		18·0	
Barley (per cwt)								
(a) Market value	19	5¾	19	8	21	9¼	20	10
(b) Unit subsidy	9	3¼	7	11	3	0¾	33	6¾
(c) Total return	28	9	27	7	24	10	24	4¾
(b) as percentage of (c)	32·0		30·0		12·0		14·0	

Source: *Annual Review and Determination of Guarantees*, HMSO, 1969.

* Rounded.

TABLE VI. *Cost of Exchequer Support to Agriculture as a Proportion of Total Exchequer Expenditure United Kingdom, 1956–7 to 1968–9*

	%
1956–7	4·8
1957–8	5·6
1960–1	4·4
1961–2	5·2
1964–5	3·4
1965–6	2·8
1967–8	2·4

Source: *Annual Review and Determination of Guarantees*, 1965 ff. (annually); *Statistical Abstract of the United Kingdom*, 1957 ff. (annually).

The result of these policies has been that exchequer expenditure on agricultural support has fallen not only as a proportion of total exchequer expenditure but absolutely (Table VI). For different products annual support calculated as a proportion of the unsupported value varies from year to year, according to the vagaries of the weather and of international trading conditions. Milk and dairy produce have the lowest level of support—about 3 per cent in 1967-8—and so of all British farm products come nearest to getting their total return from the market; the almost totally inelastic demand for liquid milk, the price of which supports that of manufactured dairy produce, makes this possible. Cereals have, in most years, the highest proportion of their total return from government support measures. Meanwhile net output has continued to rise, though with less rapidity; it now is more than double the output of British agriculture in the 1930s, and about 40 per cent above the level of the mid 1950s. British farmers produce 60 per cent of the country's temperate foodstuffs, distributed as shown in Table VII. The tightening of margins in the 1960s has been considerable; unit prices of most agricultural products have either fallen or risen only slowly, which means that in real terms they have fallen to a greater or less degree. Each year's Price Review sees an item calculated to enrage farmers; this is the 'efficiency factor', the calculation of the amount by which the increasing efficiency of the industry allows it to absorb rising costs, estimated by the Government to be about £30 million a year on an average. Sometimes the Government graciously allows farmers to retain some of the benefits of their improved efficiency; in general most of those benefits are passed on to the consumer or taxpayer: in the 1960s the average annual rise in the net income of agriculture has been 2·5 per cent while wages and salaries in the whole economy have risen annually by 6 per cent.

The British policy of price support by deficiency payments has some advantages; it allows the consumer to benefit from falls in world prices of food, and because it does not discourage consumption by high prices the poorer sections of the community benefit more than the more wealthy, who, under a progressive system of taxation, pay the costs of agricultural price support. During the 1960s some of its former disadvantages—unpredictable fluctuations in market price because of sudden influxes of (sometimes dumped) imports, with concomitant increases in the subsidy bill as long as this was 'open ended'—have been overcome by policies of negotiating market-sharing agreements with foreign suppliers, by minimum import prices, and the imposition of standard quantities. The disadvantage of the system from the farmers' point of view would seem to be the fact that the cost of agricultural support is perfectly clear, and not disguised in the consumer price, as are tariff supports. It is thus very easy to calculate the cost to the nation of agricultural support, while the benefits must remain debatable as long as world food supplies are plentiful and Britain is able to pay for them (which latter condition certainly did not obtain in the 1960s). Recent calculations have suggested that a further expansion of British agricultural output in order to reduce imports would be of benefit to the balance of payments;[1] at the present time methods of financing such an expansion are under debate. The Labour party adheres to the policy of deficiency payments; the Conservative party favours the adoption of a policy of import levies, such as would have to be adopted if Britain joins the EEC with consequent rises in food prices. The farmers

TABLE VII. *Proportion of United Kingdom Temperate Food Needs Supplied from Home Production percentage*

	1938*	1953–4	1966–7
Wheat	22·7	40·9	45·4
Barley	46·2	66·8	97·9
Beef and Veal	49·1	65·8	73·0
Pork	77·7	88·3	98·8
Bacon and ham	29·3	43·0	33·0
Mutton and lamb	35·9	35·4	43·8
Butter	8·9	9·4	6·7
Cheese	24·1	37·5	50·8
Eggs	61·8	80·2	95·6
Potatoes	95·9	97·8	94·5
Sugar	17·9	19·4	29·0

* Average of several years in 1930s.

Source: A Century of Agricultural Statistics, HMSO, 1968.

are not at all enthusiastic about the adoption of the European policy, with its 'target' rather than guaranteed prices, and have persuaded the Conservative party to supplement its levy policy with the promise of minimum guaranteed prices and a transition period in which the workings of finance by levy can be tested. At the moment when the Common Agricultural Policy of the EEC is in difficulties both because of its inability to deal with changes in international monetary values and because of its inducement of mounting surpluses, it is as well to consider whether the effects of the two policies have diverged because of inherent differences in the policies or because of different circumstances in the countries in which they operate.

[1] *Agriculture's Import Saving Role*, NEDC for Agriculture, HMSO, 1968.

The EEC and British Systems Compared

The salient relevant differences between the EEC and Britain are in the proportion of the population of each economic unit engaged in agriculture and the degree of agricultural self-sufficiency. Britain produces 50 per cent of its total food requirements with no more than 3·5 per cent of its working population engaged in farming as farmers or workers, and of these about one-eighth are part-time farmers. The EEC has 15 per cent of its working population employed in agriculture producing about 90 per cent of its food; most of these are farmers, and very small farmers too. We saw in Chapter II that scale of enterprise, which determines the amount left for investment and improvements once living costs have been met, is one of the factors influencing farming efficiency: the structure of farming in Britain is much better than in the EEC; it is therefore not surprising that the efficiency of the majority of British farmers is higher than that of the majority of farmers in the EEC and that the latter can remain in farming only if prices for agricultural commodities are set at a level very much higher than those of British farm products (Table VIII).

TABLE VIII. *Producer Prices of Agricultural Commodities in 1969, United Kingdom and EEC*

($ per 1,000 kg)

	UK	EEC
Wheat	70·0	125·00
Barley	63·0	94·44
Fat cattle	48·8	680·00
Milk	95·8	103·00
Butter	300·0	1,735·00
Skim milk powder	—	712·50
Sugar	110·0	223·50

Source: Annual Review and Determination of Guarantees, 1968, E.E.C. Spokesman's Office, Brussels, Dec 1968.

The choice before the EEC is therefore between (a) continuing a high level of farm support which will enable most of the existing farmers to stay in agriculture, or (b) reducing support and so compelling the smaller and less efficient farmers to leave the industry, or (c) a deliberate policy of re-structuring agriculture so that the remaining farmers can make a reasonable living at lower prices, while those leaving are induced to do so in a humane manner, with compensation for their loss of land and livelihood. The cost of the first and last of these policies will be considerable; present price support is costing over 2,400 million dollars a year (£1,000 million). The cost of implementing the Mansholt Plan for the re-structuring of European agriculture has been estimated at £250 million a year for five years, in addition to the necessary remaining price supports, and other financial measures to reduce the population of dairy cows. The second policy, that of forcing the withdrawal of labour from agriculture by the reduction of prices is politically unacceptable. (British onlookers should refrain from being smug about such political questions, reflecting that their own re-structuring of agriculture was achieved conveniently for the urban population in the last quarter of the nineteenth century at considerable human cost to the agricultural community, and that in other more influential sections of the community British Governments have been very circumspect in their attempts to bring about changes.)

In these circumstances the decision between types of agricultural support is seen to be taken in terms of politics, not of economics. The burden of agricultural support is as onerous in total whether it is imposed by levies or by exchequer payments; the difference is in the section of society which bears this burden. Levies raise the price of food, which adversely affects the poorer sections. Deficiency payments on the other hand are made from the taxes of the better off, and thus act as a measure of income redistribution. The proportion of national income which may be devoted to agricultural support without arousing political opposition is greater the greater the size and influence of the agricultural population; but conversely, the larger the agricultural sector, the less well *able* will be the rest of the community to bear the cost of agricultural support.

It is, therefore, unlikely that the EEC will be able to adopt the 'standard quantity' solution to the problem of surplus production and high support costs, even though this solution may be seen to have worked well in Britain in the 1960s, where with tightening margins the gradual departure of the inefficient has left a smaller but more efficient and better structured industry which has hitherto still had confidence to maintain production because of the basic security of the agricultural guarantees. Even if such a solution were adopted in the EEC, this would not necessarily reduce greatly the problem of surplus production; we saw in Chapter IV that a policy of tighter margins in, for example, British milk production, reduced numbers of producers but did not reduce output since the inefficient and smaller producers left the industry and the larger and more efficient remained. If, in a world of unequally shared national incomes, it is necessary to reduce agricultural production in some countries, this can probably be achieved only by the withdrawal of other factors of production from agriculture in addition to the with-drawal of farmers, and even such withdrawal of other factors may not reduce output, as we can see from the experience of the United States.

The United States and the Withdrawal of Resources from Agriculture

The United States has a long tradition of supporting agriculture. This began with the distribution of land either free or at very low prices in the nineteenth century, continued with the provision of agricultural education and the subsidization of capital investment by low interest rates, and continues through similar developmental policies today. The depression of 1931 caused catastrophic falls in the prices of farm products, and in 1933 the policy of control of supply and compensation to farmers was begun by the Agricultural Adjustment Act, which provided public finance for payments to farmers who agreed to limit the acreage of certain crops, for the substitution of soil-conserving crops for others less desirable, and for a system of deficiency payments to make up the difference between the prices received by farmers and parity prices. ('Parity' means the relation between the prices paid by and received by farmers, based on the period 1910–14 as the norm.) These policies were meant to be temporary, but they are still in operation. For many years their success has been limited by the improvements in technology which enabled more food to be produced from fewer acres, and by the tendency of participating farmers to take their worst land out of production and to concentrate their efforts on the best land.

From the beginning, programmes of withdrawal were supple-mented by support buying; the Commodity Credit Corporation was set up in 1933 to make loans to farmers when the prices of crops fell below parity; the loans were made after harvest and ran from six to eight months. If prices rose, farmers could sell their crop and redeem their loan; if at the end of the loan period prices were still below parity, the CCC would buy the crop and store it. It thus operates a buffer policy. During the 1930s the CCC accumulated huge stocks, and though these were disposed of in the years of war, and again in the Korean crisis of 1951–2, they had accumulated again by the mid 1950s, when the passing of Public Law 480 legalized concessionary sales to developing countries. Disposals of food grains under this law in the years of shortage in the mid 1960s reduced stocks to their lowest acceptable strategic level, but they have again mounted.

The United States Government is therefore turning increasingly to policies of withdrawal of land from farming under long-term contracts, and the active promotion of alternative land uses in forestry, recreational enterprises, soil-conservation programmes and the like. Of current government expenditure on farm support programmes, about one-fifth now goes to farmers in direct payment for taking land out of production; the other four-fifths are divided more or less equally between financing the price support programmes of the ccc and the disposal of surpluses.

The limitations of this method of control of supply lie in the increasingly profitable substitution of capital for land and labour; with less than half its peak number of workers and farms, with 20 million hectares withdrawn from production (about $4\frac{1}{2}$ per cent of land in farms, and nearly twice the agricultural area of England and Wales) farm output steadily rises; by 1967 it was 18 per cent above its level of ten years previously. It has been estimated that by 1980 United States Agriculture could produce surpluses with as few as 700,000 farms instead of the present 3 million, and a labour force of 2·5 million instead of the 6 million persons now employed in agriculture. This is entirely credible, given physical and technical conditions in which one man, with $11,000 worth of casual labour at busy times, can farm 1,300 acres with a specially pepped-up tractor and suitable implements.[2]

Future Policies

In considering future policies for agriculture, it is important to make explicit the assumptions about future patterns of world development on which such policies are based. It is, for example, futile to discuss the development of agriculture in Britain in terms of, say, reducing government agricultural support and letting farms in many parts of the country become playgrounds for urban holiday-makers unless it is made clear that such a policy would require the continuance of measures of government support for agriculture in other countries, so that Britain could continue to enjoy the benefits of cheap food subsidized by the nationals of other lands. How far other countries will be willing to provide cheap food for Britain as a by-product of supporting their own farmers is not a question which can confidently be answered; nor can a policy based on such assumptions be other than one of very restricted application. Not every country can economically afford to adopt such a policy, even if it were politically feasible.

There are, however, some common factors in the agriculture of Western countries which make it possible to distinguish certain lines

[2] *Farm Journal*, November 1969.

of future policy which might be of general application. It is certain that, with modern techniques, farmers in the countries of Western Europe and America can produce far more food than those countries as a whole can consume. For the world as a whole the picture may be far different; this we do not know, for while demographers are unanimous in predicting a steep rise in world population, agriculturalists are far from unanimous in assessing the capacity of the world's agricultures to feed the new mouths even on the low standards which prevail over much of the presently undeveloped world. On the one hand it therefore seems immoral to attempt to stem the flood of agricultural production in the Western world, since we cannot say that in the future the 'surpluses' will not become, as they did in 1966 and 1967, very necessary stockpiles. On the other hand, the developing countries will not choose to be indefinitely receivers of food aid if they can, from their own resources, produce enough to provide an acceptable standard of nutrition for their peoples; this will depend on their command of capital as well as on their technological progress. The possibility of the developing nations becoming customers in world markets for food produced in the West is also doubtful; only the oil sheikdoms seem, at the present time, to be assured of enough foreign exchange to make this likely. It is therefore probable that Western governments will, within the limits of the politically acceptable, attempt to limit the support which they give to their own agriculture by protection or subsidy and to withdraw resources from agriculture to some degree.

We have seen, however, earlier in this chapter and in Chapter IV that the withdrawal of one resource may simply lead to the substitution of another and to no fall in output; this is especially true of the substitution of capital for labour and land. Capital itself must be withdrawn from agriculture if production is to be decreased or held at its present level. In the past, the withdrawal of capital from agriculture has come about as the result of falling incomes. Farmers begin to economize on variable inputs as incomes fall; they use less fertilizer, less hired labour, poorer seed and cut out expenditure on the maintenance of buildings and plant. Output falls; land and fixed capital deteriorate; incomes fall still further, till the servicing of loans becomes impossible and the impoverished farmers sell out to more prosperous neighbours at prices which will enable the latter to farm extensively, putting little into the land and getting little out of it. The results of this process may be seen in marginal farming areas; in the United States in the Appalachians and in parts of the South, for instance, and in Britain in the highland areas of Scotland, Wales and northern England.

During this process there is much impoverishment of the whole rural community, not only of farmers but of those in agriculture's ancillary trades and in the service trades. There is a movement away from such declining rural areas; nobody wants to live in a place where schools are small or too far away, where there are no career opportunities for their children, where social life is restricted, where public transport is non-existent or so intermittent as to be useless for shopping, social activities or journey to work. Such areas of rural decay do not strike the eye as do the decaying parts of towns; there may be some empty houses, or some which though apparently inhabited are simply used as holiday homes, but the houses that are lived in will be properly maintained and will not have the outward and visible signs of material decay. In Britain the places concerned are often those most admired by town dwellers in search of recreation; these see 'stark grandeur' in the eroded landscapes characteristic of the century-long monoculture of sheep, as in the English Lake District and the Scottish Highlands, and in the tree-denuded sour pastures of much of the Pennines. Whatever spiritual graces post-Wordsworthian man may receive from the highlands, for their inhabitants they may be as much places of deprivation as any but the worst quarters of cities.

The alternative to this depressing process of unplanned capital withdrawal is that of the planned substitution of opportunities in non-agricultural occupations as agriculture contracts. This is a more complex matter than simply that of the pensioning off of old or unsuccessful farmers and the amalgamation of farms, which are the measures generally accepted as applicable to the problem sectors of agriculture. Amalgamation alone may simply produce areas of social decay even where agriculture itself is thriving, as in, for example, the Lincolnshire Wolds, where increasing prosperity in agriculture has been accompanied by a decline in village populations and in rural services. In the past a prosperous agriculture was sufficiently labour-intensive to maintain viable communities, both in the sense of making possible the maintenance of services and the more nebulous sense of producing by a common interest neighbourhoods with a feeling of security and cohesion. Neither decaying marginal farming nor prosperous capital-intensive farming can do this; people are simply too thin on the ground.

The problem which agricultural policies must attempt to solve is, therefore, not only that of withdrawing resources from agriculture but also that of replacing agriculture, or supplementing it, to provide a secure social and economic base for rural areas. Some years ago it was thought that forestry would be capable, in hill areas, of providing such a substitute, but modern forestry shares with modern agriculture a trend towards increasing mechanization, so that forestry may well need no more labour per hectare than mechanized lowland farming, and will be no more capable than agriculture of sustaining the social and economic fabric of rural areas, even where it is to be preferred on land usage grounds.

One possibility which has been canvassed is that of treating regions of productive land as predominantly farming areas, with the emphasis on intensive production, while the higher and marginal areas are treated as primarily places of recreation, with such farmers as remain engaged in providing services for tourists. This may certainly be a solution for some farms, but there are considerable difficulties in making the assumption that all hill farmers and their wives are necessarily good caterers, and in gearing the level of agricultural support for such areas to the premise that farmers supplement their incomes from agriculture with that from tourism. In general, except where both winter and summer seasons are possible, tourism based on the natural attractions of the countryside is not capable of replacing agriculture as the economic base of a region, being at once largely female-employing and highly seasonal. As an ancillary occupation it has its uses, particularly as opportunities for female employment are few in the more remote areas.

Paradoxically, it is probably the dispersion of industry into rural areas which at once offers the best prospect of retaining an adequate rural population and at the same time achieving the structural transformation of agriculture and the transference of resources that will be needed if incomes in farming are to compare not too unfavourably with those in other sectors of the economy. When young farmers and farm workers see their contemporaries taking home full wage packets from factories in local towns many of them opt for a change of employment more easily than when this would entail migration. Improved transport makes the disadvantages of dispersion progressively less severe to a wide range of industry, and the advantages to the rural areas are obvious, as can be seen when a thriving rural district with a good centre of employment is compared with one, perhaps no more than twenty miles away, with no work opportunities outside agriculture. In this context government policies for assisted farm amalgamation make sense; without it purely agricultural regions will suffer from the inadequacies of too narrow an economic and social base, and the low incomes that accompany the 'stickiness' of factors of production in agriculture.

SUGGESTIONS FOR FURTHER READING
(additional to those referred to in the text)

Annual Series
EEC, *Statistique Agricole.*
FAO, *The State of Food and Agriculture.*
   Production Yearbooks.
   Trade Yearbooks.
HMSO, *Agricultural Statistics.*
Milk Marketing Board, *Dairy Facts and Figures.*
   Yearbook of Agricultural Co-operation.
USDA, *Agricultural Statistics.*

Official Publications
Commonwealth Agricultural Committee, *Commodity Reports.*
HMSO, *The Structure of Agriculture*, 1966.
   Report of the Land Use Study Group, 1966.
   A Century of Agricultural Statistics, 1866–1966, 1967.
   Agriculture's Import Saving Role, NEDC for Agriculture, 1968.
OECD, *Low Incomes in Agriculture*, Paris, 1961.
   Inter-relationships between Income and Supply Problems in Agriculture, Paris, 1965.
   Agricultural Policies in 1966, Paris, 1967.

Secondary Sources
ALLEN, G. R., *Agricultural Marketing Policies*, Blackwell, Oxford, 1959.
ASHTON, J. and ROGERS, S. eds., *Economic Change and Agriculture*, Oliver and Boyd, London, 1967.
BUTTERWICK, M. and ROLFE, E., *Food, Farming and the Common Market*, Oxford University Press, 1968.
DIGBY, M., *Agricultural Co-operation in the United Kingdom*, Plunkett Foundation for Co-operative Studies, Occasional Paper No. 34.
EICHER and WITT eds., *Agriculture in Economic Development*, McGraw Hill, 1964.
HALLET, G., *The Economics of Agricultural Policy*, Blackwell, 1968.
HEADY, EARL O. and TWEETEN, L., *Resource Demand and Structure of the Agricultural Industry*, Iowa State University Press, 1963.
HOUSE, J. W., *Rural North-East England*, University of Newcastle-on-Tyne, 1965.

McCRONE, G., *The Economics of Subsidizing Agriculture*, Allen and Unwin, London, 1962.

PREBISCH, R., *Towards a New Trade Policy for Development*, UN, 1964.

SCOTT WATSON, J. ed., *Agriculture in the British Economy*, ICI, 1957.

TRACY, M., *Agriculture in Western Europe*, Jonathan Cape, London, 1964.

WIBBERLEY, G. P., *Recreation and the Countryside*, Manchester Statistical Society, 1966.

QUEEN MARY
COLLEGE
LIBRARY

INDEX

161